What Others Are Saying about This Book . . .

"This is a methodical, well-informed, easy-to-read, and concise collection of teaching techniques used by Jesus Himself along with a very practical understanding of the related sources from scripture. It is a wonderful resource for homily preparation as well as a necessary guide for catechesis. Truly a useful resource for one in ministry."

~ **Deacon Denzil Lobo** *Madison, Mississippi*

"What I keep learning from this book is that great teaching is not about being the smartest person in the room with all the right answers; it is about joyfully sharing your faith through stories, questions, actions, and conversation. A masterful and poetic bringing together of scripture and instruction with a vision of sharing faith that will re-inspire you every time you pick it up. Highly recommended!"

~ **Blake Sittler** *Director of Pastoral Services, Saskatoon Diocese, Saskatchewan, Canada*

"Sr. Regina's book reminds us that Jesus was, first and foremost, a teacher. So as classroom teachers, catechists, administrators, or other teachers of any kind, we can look back on His life to learn how to teach from the Master. After reading *"Go Teach!"* I have a new perspective on my students, my teaching, and myself."

~ **Mary Kay O'Malley** *Assistant Principal, St. Francis of Assisi School, Gates Mills, Ohio*

"As a catechist for grades one through nine, I found myriad connections that complement and support lessons at all levels. Whether it's preparing students for receiving the sacraments of the Holy Eucharist or Confirmation, and everything in between, this book provides a practical roadmap teachers can readily use to inspire the messages we strive to impart to God's children."

~ **Carol Kapostasy** *Catechist, St. Mark the Evangelist, Fort Pierce, Florida*

"With no modern-day technology to assist him, Jesus taught groups large and small with a mastery that resonates to this day. Sister Regina Alfonso shares in poetic fashion the artfulness of Jesus as a master teacher and how we might draw upon his skills for both inspiration and imitation. New and seasoned catechists and Catholic school teachers will find much to reflect upon as they move through this book— both for mastering their own skills and for deepening their understanding and appreciation of Jesus' teachings."

~ **Kathy Hendricks** National Catechetical Consultant, William H. Sadlier

"I was completely hooked after the first chapter. It's a charming, enlightening, inspiring "Bible study" from a very unique perspective. Copies will no doubt be dog-eared by the end of the school year."

~ **Paula Aveni** *Director,*
SND National Education Office

Regina Alfonso reminded me that Jesus didn't just give us a powerful message to spread to the world; he also gave us through his example the teaching methods necessary to spread that message successfully. She breaks down these methods in a way that is timeless, inspirational, and practical. A well-researched and well-written book."

~ **Amanda Haberman** *Parish School of Religion Coordinator, St. Dominic School, Shaker Heights, Ohio*

"The beauty of *"Go Teach!" And Jesus Showed Us How* is that it provides teachers with a tool that is relevant and informative yet at the same time calls for reflection. Each key point references a specific scripture passage assisting educators in making a direct connection between the teachings of Jesus and student learning."

~ **Jennifer Massiello** *Assistant Principal, Notre Dame Elementary School, Chardon, Ohio*

"GO TEACH!"

And Jesus Showed Us How

"GO TEACH!"

And Jesus Showed Us How

Joyce,
may God bless you
and your ministry.
S. Regina Alfonso, SND

REGINA ALFONSO, SND

✳ ✳ ✳
. . . .

ILLUSTRATED BY MARIE FIHN, SND

Edited and formatted by Mary Kathleen Glavich, SND
Interior art by Marie Fihn, SND
Cover art by Carl Heinrich Bloch
Photo on page 155 by Mary Barbara Daugherty, SND

ISBN-13: 978-1542529624
ISBN-10: 154252962X

Printed in the United States of America

DEDICATION

To all who have taught me,
especially my first and best teachers

Joseph M. Alfonso, Sr., and Aldemira Benedetti Alfonso

and to all the students
I have been privileged to teach

Contents

FOREWARD

In the Gospels, Jesus is addressed as Teacher more than any other title. His career, or public ministry, was education. He taught about God, the kingdom of God, himself, and how to live on earth so as to live eternally in heaven. As he taught, "the crowds were astounded at his teaching" (Matthew 7:28). As typical of teachers, or masters, at the time, he attracted disciples, a group of followers who learned and memorized his teachings and passed them on. These original students were taught so well that now, some two thousand years later, the teachings of Jesus are well known. What other teacher has had such success?

Then it makes sense for teachers today to look to Jesus as a model or mentor. True, he did not have modern teaching tools like Smartboards, iPads, and videos. He didn't even have textbooks! Still, the simple methods he used in first-century Israel and the principles on which they are founded can touch the hearts and form the lives of students of all centuries and countries. Aware of this, Sister Regina wrote this book for teachers, drawing on the example of Jesus as teacher.

Each part presents teaching moments in the life of Jesus that illustrate a particular method, such as using concrete objects, storytelling, and questioning. These are followed by practical pointers for teachers as they imitate his style. Throughout the book, the author wisely emphasizes what someone observed: "The mediocre teacher tells. The good teacher explains. The superior teacher demonstrates. The great teacher inspires."

But beyond being a mini-methods course, *"Go Teach!"* is a prayer book, a meditation book that can nurture one's relationship with Jesus. The sense line format of the text invites the reader to slow down and reflect on Jesus. Scripture citations are provided in the margins for those who wish to open their Bible for a closer look at the teaching events in his life.

I can't think of anyone more qualified to write a book on this topic. Sister Regina is a member of a religious congregation whose mission described in its Constitutions is to "serve people . . . through education and other ministries" and "place special emphasis on catechesis." For decades she has devoted herself with passion to teaching youngsters and to forming catechists. Among other things, this Sister has taught methods courses for years at Notre Dame College of Ohio, worked on a religion textbook series, flew to Uganda to expand the methods of teachers there, and now, while in her eighties, presents a lecture on methods each year at the Cleveland diocesan seminary.

Reading *"Go Teach!"* is a delightful experience. Gospel stories are retold with a creative twist. What could be dry text is not because of the occasional unexpected remarks and flashes of humor. Knowing Sister Regina, on every page I can hear her voice and picture the twinkle in her eye.

The original version of this book, published in 1986, is dead, but it still appears on the Amazon website. In 2016, a reviewer wrote: "Too bad this is out of print. I would order one for each of my catechists if I could get enough." This person will be happy to know that, thanks to Sister Regina's indefatigable commitment to teaching, her book is again alive. So will any teacher, principal, and Director of Religious Education who reads it.

Mary Kathleen Glavich, SND,
author of *The Six Tasks of Catechesis*

PREFACE

*'Will you prepare and teach a religion methods course
that will do more than just prepare prospective teachers
for teaching religion? Can you make the content
applicable for teaching everything?"*

That request, which Sister Mary Christopher made
to me in 1972, was the seed that grew into the book of
reflections in your hands. By 1986, the content of the
syllabus for my methods courses, presentations, and a
retreat became a book published by Alba House:

*How Jesus Taught:
The Methods and Techniques of the Master.*

This small volume, the result of twelve years of
Scripture-combing, was a thirty-six-year veteran teacher's
study of the methods and techniques of Jesus, and my
thoughts about how to apply them. Since that book is now
out of print and unavailable to people who wished to give
copies to their teachers, I decided to republish it with
updated language and expanded content.
This second edition,

"Go Teach!" And Jesus Showed Us How,

is also intended to share with all teachers an in-depth look at
Jesus as he taught. His methods are as effective today as
they were when he first used them two thousand years ago.
Each part of this book contains brief retellings of
Scripture accounts of Jesus' teaching encounters, followed
by practical applications to current situations. I chose to set
the thoughts in sense lines instead of block paragraphs in
order to encourage *pondering and applying the content,*
rather than just *reading* it.

My intention is to affect the education of children and young people by sharing these reflections with their teachers: Christian catechists, instructors in teacher-education programs, preK–12 teachers in all fields of studies, parents who homeschool their children, and anyone else involved in educating our next generation.

I am grateful to Mary Kathleen Glavich, SND, who edited and formatted the book, and to a fine group of readers who shared their thoughts about the manuscript: Carol Kapostasy, Deacon Denzil Lobo, Mary Agnes O'Malley, SND; Mary Kay O'Malley; and Sherry Sullin. I'm also indebted to Paula Aveni for her excellent proofreading.

But, had it not been for the request made forty-four years ago, by Mary Christopher Rohner, SND, this book would not exist.

Finally, a suggestion for you who will be reading about the methods and techniques of Jesus—

Pray this daily:

> *Bless all the students I am teaching,*
> *those I have taught, and those I will ever teach.*

Then someday you'll be able to say to a class,

"I've been praying for you since before you were born."

Regina Alfonso, SND
January 26, 2017

.

INTRODUCTION

Imagine yourself with the prospect of choosing a small, elite band of twelve students to become the nucleus of the first school of its kind. This school will be uniquely designed to initiate a new way of life, built on some very revolutionary principles. Suppose, too, that your most valuable personal characteristic is the fact that you can read the heart and mind of every person.

Wouldn't you select the most capable, qualified twelve you can find within the population of about 21,000 square miles? What teacher wouldn't make the most of such an opportunity to select super-students for the core of that exceptional school!

* * *   * * *   * * *

Those were the facts when the Master Teacher selected his Twelve. Considering all this, he made some very surprising choices. He picked . . .

✧ one who would become famous for his doubting, another for his denials, and a third for his despair
✧ two of whom would simply appear on the roster, never having said or done anything distinctive enough to be recorded
✧ one who would be embarrassed when recognized as a member of the Twelve, who would need the help of another to write his own memoirs
✧ two sets of fishermen brothers who worked well as a team
✧ two fiery-tempered students whose attitudes would require some strong reprimands
✧ a tax collector of questionable reputation
✧ a political patriot, the mystery apostle
✧ one who would never totally accept the teacher's philosophy and who would trigger the events leading to the death of the Master and to his own.

On the surface,
not a very promising group!
　　But he had confidence in them;
　　he knew their potential for growth
　　　　even though it wouldn't be very obvious to others
　　　　during their years of schooling.

　　But, just think of the effects of that educational system!

The giftedness of each of the Twelve continues to unfold
　　as his mission is accomplished
　　by students of his students
　　　　two thousand years later.

Talk about retention! Talk about learning outcomes!
　　How did he do it?

A close scrutiny of the Gospels
　　reveals Jesus utilizing all the teaching strategies
　　　　modern educators have "invented,"
　　and applying the latest discoveries and theories
　　　　of equally modern psychologists.

He is just as successful
　　in both large and small group instruction
　　　　as he is in modified departmentalized
　　　　　　and team teaching arrangements.
　　Here, individualized instruction appears at its finest.

And the wide variety of techniques
　　he uses with all his students
　　　　is awesome!

Although there doesn't seem to be any indication
　　that he ever wrote a daily lesson plan
　　or a long-range unit,
　　　　he is prepared to the hilt
　　　　　for each encounter with his students,
　　　　　　　whether he meets them
　　　　　　　　by the thousands
　　　　　　　　or one at a time.

He handles teaching aids effectively.
He holds a challenging parent-teacher conference.
He takes his homeroom group on field trips,
    and corrects them
        with both humor and sternness.

He gives directions
    (and repeats them several times);
        and he adapts his teaching
        to at least seventeen different settings
        — some of them less than ideal!

His procedures
    in "the September" of his career
    are noticeably different from those
he uses in the "June" of it.

He adjusts and adapts to slower students and to gifted ones.
He varies his plans
    as he faces reluctant learners and eager ones,
        the frightened and the bold ones,
        the naïve ones
        and those who shield their phoniness
        with masks.

In summary,
    Jesus confronts the same situations and problems
    that today's teacher faces.

And he has the solutions,
    ready to share with anyone
    who takes the time
        to examine and reflect.

PART ONE

LARGE GROUP INSTRUCTION

LARGE GROUP INSTRUCTION

At least twice
    Jesus' class numbered 4000 or 5000 men,
    plus, who knows how many women and children?
    And the Gospels state that a few other times
    he taught "crowds."

His techniques in dealing
with the crowds that followed him
    should give plenty of suggestions
        for teaching a class in September;
for the qualities of a crowd
    are quite similar to those
        of the class we face
        in the beginning of the year,
        before personalities
        have had a chance to jell
        into a cohesive team.

The individuals in his motley crowd
    differed in cultural and political backgrounds,
        in attention spans,
        and even in their purposes
        for being present in that gathering.

Though many must have been there
    because of sincere interest
    and desire to learn,
        how many others had come
        to satisfy curiosity
        or to entrap the speaker?

How many came
    because there was nothing else to do,
    or perhaps at the invitation of a friend?

And there probably were at least some
    easily distracted young people among them:

    "Because my mother made me come."

Jesus must have been encouraged
    as he looked into eager eyes
        enthralled with his Good News.
And perhaps he felt a bit annoyed
    as he noticed animated business transactions
    on the outskirts of the crowd.

However, the sight of darting, giggling youngsters
    playing tag among the long robes
        and sandaled feet of his audience
        would have pleased him,
    since he never tried to teach them.

        He simply blessed them
        and left their instruction
        to their parents!

Jesus faced people
    of all ages and mental abilities,
        all degrees of education
        and lack of it.

And what did he do?
Mostly, he told parables about
    wineskins,
        blind men,
            wedding feasts,
               seeds,
                  coins,
                     and patches.

With few exceptions,
    Jesus seemed to save the longer
    and more complex parables
      for his smaller groups.

Most of his "crowd" parables
    were only one, two,
    or three verses worth of thought.

Maybe, due to the lack of an amplifying system,
    the thoughts had to be rippled through the thousands
    because of the repetition of

"What did he say? I couldn't quite hear him!"

But the content of the few sentences
    in each brief parable
    is worth looking at.

Examine some of these in detail:

House builders	Lk 6:47-49
Hidden treasure	Mt 13:44
Lamp on a lampstand	Lk 8:16-18
Mustard seed	Mt 13:31-32
Patches on cloth	Mt 9:16
Pearl	Mt 13:45-46
Wedding feast	Mt 9:15
Yeast	Lk 13:20-21
Worthless salt	Mk 9:50

Each one is short,
    to the point,
        and connects
            a common everyday item or experience
                to an eternal truth.

And the result?

Several times a week,
    while up to their elbows in flour,
    women worked a bit of yeast
        into some soft dough
    and pondered a truth
        greater than rising bread.

        * * *   * * *   * * *

In the Gospels, Jesus used
    a very long lecture with the crowds
    only a couple of times.
And in one case,
    the results were disastrous!   Jn 6:48-60

For twenty-eight verses
    he explained about himself
        as the Bread of Life . . .
        intense, heavy expounding,
        evidently ignoring the lack of readiness
        of at least some of his students.

He should have caught a message
    when the squirming sundial watchers
        among the group
        began to fidget.

    "This teaching is too hard. Who can listen to this?"

But he was so caught up
    in the importance of the thought
        that he charged ahead
        for another five verses!
And John notes, rather bluntly, in verse sixty-six:

    "Because of this, many of his followers turned back
        and would not go with him anymore."

Long, heavy lectures,
    with no breaks or change of activities,
        tend to turn out that way.

Maybe he tried it
   to show us what to avoid.

     * * *   * * *   * * *

The crowd method
   that he seemed to rely on
   even more than pithy parables
   and long lectures
      was his own personal example.

The townspeople of Nain   Lk 7:11-15
   in the funeral procession
     were awestruck
      as they watched the Teacher
     console the grieving widow
     as none of them could do.

Thousands
   saw him concerned enough
   about their hunger
      to feed them.   Mt 14:13-21
They were impressed
    with his miracles
        to alleviate suffering,   Mt 8:5-13
    with his fearlessness
      in dealing with hypocrisy,
    with his gentleness   Lk 12:1-3
      with children   Mk 10:13-16
       and outcasts   Lk 5:12-16
        and sinners.   Jn 8: 1-11

And, by his own heroic acceptance
   of his Father's will
     in the Passion,

he taught all who wished to learn
   how to accept humiliation,
     physical and mental suffering,
     and even death.

—

27

And NOW
when we teach our "crowds" . . .

Parables

With our instant mixes
    and twenty-lane freeways,
        his parable method still works,
            but not so well using yeast
                and fig trees.

How essential it is that teachers
know thoroughly
    what is truly common and everyday
        in the lives of their students:
            — about afterschool hangouts and hobbies
            — about popular fads and fashions
            — about sports and current TV and movie fare
            — about momentary heroes and assorted stars.

We can't create memorable parables
    if we don't know what's important
    to our students.

Our current "yeast"
    must be just as attention-grabbing
    as the images he used.

Long Lectures

Younger students,
    and slower ones
    have a very short attention span.
(Older ones and brighter ones
    aren't really much different.)

Long-winded teacher explanations
    are guaranteed
    to create disciplinary problems
        as one listener after another
           reaches the end
           of power-to-concentrate.

Ten minutes is a *L-O-N-G* time unless
    a. the teacher is dynamic
    b. the topic is novel
    c. the students are enthralled.

And, if a, or b, or c is missing
        the concentration time
        is proportionately shortened.

The seriousness
    of the disciplinary problems
    that will follow
        will depend upon the age and ingenuity
           of the students,
        and the ability
           of the teacher
               to change activities
               at the first glint of distraction
                  in the eye
                  of the first turned-off student.

If we must explain,
    —and sometimes we must—
 it's good to involve the students
 in helping to explain,
        contributing as much as they know.
 We can fill in gaps,
    adeptly stringing together
        the students' contributions
        into a logical framework.

The more they own the explanation,
    the less likely they are
        to "run out of listen."

It's been said that the *minutes*
    of a student's attention span
        equals
    the *student's age*
       plus three.
  . . . Might be worth considering when teaching.

Personal Example

It's an old saying,
    but it's frighteningly true:
"Your actions shout so loudly that I can't hear your words."

What do we want our students to be?
    honest?   kind?
        generous?   truthful?
            unselfish?   joyous?
                courteous?   obedient?
                compassionate?   prayerful?

Are they seeing these traits in their teacher
    as they watch us deal with
        their classmates?
        their families?
            the parish community?
                the rest of the faculty?
                the administrators?
                  the maintenance crew?

If they SEE what we mean
    when we TELL them,
there's a 50/50 chance
    they might choose to live
        a Christian life.

If they don't see in us
    what we tell them,
        the chances dwindle
            a lot.

PART TWO

INDIVIDUALIZED INSTRUCTION

Nicodemus

INDIVIDUALIZED INSTRUCTION

Teachers who examine the encounters of Jesus with individuals will find themselves distracted by the many similarities between Jesus' students and their own. A closer meditative focus on a sampling reveals how his techniques matched the background, the readiness, and the need of each student.

Diamond in the Rough

Matthew gives us the basic facts
about his momentous encounter
with the Master.

It must have looked casual
and spontaneous, that first meeting.
Jesus saw the tax collector in his office,
leaving no doubt as to his profession.

In spite of this,
or maybe because of it,
Jesus said to him:
"Follow Me."

And he did.   Mt 9:9-13

To celebrate the occasion,
Matthew hosted a dinner.
Luke stretches it to a "big feast."

Besides Jesus and his other new disciples,
Matthew also invited his friends,
his tax-collector buddies,
and an assortment of other outcasts.

Shocked to find such a gathering of riffraff
    eating with the Teacher,
        the Pharisees questioned his disciples,
           probably with raised eyebrows,
             and noses in the air.

And Jesus came to the defense
    of his tax collector
        who would record the life of the Teacher
        and give his life
           for him and his Good News.

"I have not come
    to call the respectable people to repent,
    but the outcasts."   Lk 5:27-32

And NOW
when we teach our diamonds . . .

✧ We need to be aware
    that potential may be covered
    by a questionable reputation
    or undesirable actions.

✧ Our diamonds need to know
    that we value them
    and see that potential.

✧ Sometimes we need to speak up in their defense,
    even in the faculty room.

✧ Jesus was never reluctant
    to be associated with diamonds in the rough.

    Neither should we be.

The Insecure

Thirty-eight years of doing nothing
    but lying on a mat
        would wipe out anybody's self-confidence.
        It could also provide plenty of support
            for insecurity.

And the Teacher knew that.
    Perhaps that's why Jesus' first words
        to the paralytic were:

        "Do you *want* to get well?"

The poor fellow's response
    held more than a trace of doubt
        and a whimpering self-pity:

            "Sir, I don't have anyone here
                to put me in the pool
                when the water is stirred up.

            While I am trying to get in,
                somebody else gets there first."

Jesus offered him no sympathy;
    didn't even stretch out a hand
        to help him up.

His words were
    a *command to be independent*:

        "Get up, pick up your mat, and walk."
        You don't need anybody from now on.

And later
    when Jesus saw him again,
        he reaffirmed that independence.   Jn 5:1-18

And NOW
when we teach our insecure ones . . .

✧ Never do for students what they can do for themselves.

✧ Challenge each student to become independent of you.

✧ Create opportunities for students to prove themselves
   to themselves.

✧ Support with encouragement: "I knew you could do it."

✧ Group students for learning projects and activities
      to increase their awareness of opportunities
         to appreciate others' talents
         and to assist one another.

           * * *   * * *   * * *
           . . . .

The Experimenter

Peter and the others were frightened enough
      by the predawn storm,
            but the appearance of "the ghost"
                  was just too much!

Only the sound of his voice
      and his usual message:
            "Courage! It is I. Don't be afraid,"
                  put some degree of calm into them.

It was more than a relief to Peter.
It was a challenge.
      "Lord, if it is really you,
            order me to come out
            on the water to you."

And with one word: "Come!"
permission was merged with encouragement.

Jesus gave Peter no warnings,
no directions,
no suggestions.
He merely kept an eye
on the eager experimenter.

He was aware of Peter's fuzzy frame of faith;
he certainly saw the feet sinking
and the eyes stretched wide in fright.

But *he waited*
until his brave student called for help
before he reached out to grab him.
"Save me, Lord!"

Even as he hoisted Peter into the boat,
he offered a bit more encouragement:
"Why did you doubt?"
We could have done it together.   Mt 14:25-33

And NOW
when we teach our experimenters . . .

✧ Create a setting for independent exploration.

✧ Be there, just in case.

✧ Build confidence by showing confidence.

✧ Be conscious of the ordinariness of mistakes
during the early stages of learning,
and share that information with students.
It lessens the sharpness of discouragement
that accompanies little failures.

37

The Eager

The prospects of a thirteenth apostle
    really looked promising.

The young fellow wanted to know
    all about entering the Kingdom.
        "What must I do to receive eternal life?"

He heard Jesus' answer
    and felt encouraged;
    but this student really wanted a challenge.

Commandments?
He'd been living those;
    so, "What else do I need?"

Jesus was as eager in his answers
    as the young man was in his questions.

And the next two verses,
    especially the space between them,
        hold some thoughts worth pondering.

Verse twenty-two tells us
    that the young man went away sad,
        disappointed when he realized
            that using the newfound knowledge
        would alter his lifestyle.

The very next words:
    "Jesus looked around at his disciples and said…"
    tell us what Jesus *didn't* say.

He didn't call after the almost-apostle
        "Could you sell at least some of your things?"
        "How about giving part of your money to the poor?"

He didn't compromise his message
    to gain a disciple.   Mk 10:17-21; Mt 19:16-23

—

38

And NOW
when we teach our eager ones . . .

✧ Straightforward, honest questions
    deserve straightforward, honest answers.

✧ Eager students need challenges,
    opportunities that stretch their capacity.

✧ Offer content just a *bit harder*
    than they think they can accomplish
      without warning about the increased difficulty.

✧ Suggest no compromise with his message . . .

    That message is not to be watered down
    and adapted to current lifestyles.

    On the contrary,
      lifestyles are to be shaped
      to fit the message.

* * *   * * *   * * *

The Discouraged

Long faces,
    slumped shoulders,
      pace slowed by dejected spirits . . .

It didn't take long for him
    to overtake them
      on the way out of Jerusalem

    and walk along with them
      and teach them,
        though they didn't recognize him.

An all-knowing God asked:

"What are you talking about?"

and then paid very close attention
as they detailed the cause of their misery.

Only after he had drawn the problem
from them
did he explain in even greater detail
everything necessary
to bolster their courage
and their faith.

He let himself be persuaded
to stay for supper,
and some more talk.

And *only after* discouragement
had released them
did he leave them.   Lk 24:13-35

And NOW
when we teach our discouraged ones . . .

✧ Recognize the signs of discouragement.

✧ Create a simple opening for talk.

✧ Listen attentively to every detail.

✧ Encourage with facts.

✧ Stay with them until
they've conquered discouragement.

The Humiliated

A woman in disgrace
    was brought before him.

She had been
    "caught in the very act of adultery"
      (evidently by self-righteous peeping Toms).

Her shocked accusers
    were horrified by the scandal.

And the woman,
    not only obviously aware of her shame,
    but abandoned by her family,
      her friends,
      and especially by her lover,
    silently faced the inevitability
    of being stoned.

And what did he do about it all?

He really seemed to ignore her
    until he had cleverly dispersed
    her accusers.

Only then did he quietly speak to her.

He gave her no sermon.
    She didn't need it.
    She was fully conscious of her guilt.

A gentle,

    "Well, then I do not condemn you either.
      Go, but do not sin again."

        was sufficient.   Jn 8:1-11

And NOW
when we teach our humiliated ones . . .

✧ Recall the purpose of correction:
— to instruct,
— to lead to *self-control*,
— to assist the student
   in analyzing personal behavior
   and the attitudes that produced it.

✧ Correct in private:
If the offense was public,
   others need only be aware
      that correction is being made.

✧ Speak in quiet, gentle tones.

✧ Never correct to get even with the offender,
   to prove your power,
   or to use the offender as an example.

* * *   * * *   * * *
. . . .

The Masked

Jesus sat in the noonday sun
at Jacob's well
      waiting for the woman
      who wore a mask of indifference.

Had she been as nonchalant as she tried to appear,
she would have come to the well
      in the morning
            when the other village women
            gathered to draw water
                  and exchange local gossip.

42

At noon,
    the well was deserted.
No cold stares,
    or hissing whispers
    carefully planted within earshot.

She didn't seem embarrassed
    at being addressed by a strange man,
    or at a loss for words in conversing with him.

    That, evidently had never been
      much a problem
        for her.

He first asked her for a drink of water;
    and, in what must have sounded to her
      like useless banter,
        the Teacher gradually led her unwittingly
        to ask him
          for *Living Water.*

And, with one more slight turn of words,
    he asked her to call her husband.

Her response,
    "I don't have a husband,"
      was perfect.
        Which one?

No accusations,
    no humiliating words,
      only praise
        for this element of good in her:
He commended her for her truthfulness.

    "You are right
    when you say you don't have a husband . . . .
    You have told me the truth."

It's interesting to note
    that as she quickly changed the subject
    to a discussion on the best place to worship,
        Jesus didn't bring her attention back
        to her questionable lifestyle.

        No point in beating in the lesson
        when it's obviously been caught
          and flung away in shame.

He followed her lead
    and instructed her in worship,
    lifting her spiritually
        to a level she must have craved.

This brazen, adulterous hussy
    became the first woman missionary
        as she forgot her water pot
        and ran to collect her neighbors
        to bring them
        to the Good News.   Jn 4:5-30

And NOW
when we teach our masked ones . . .

✧ A simple request for a favor makes a good opener.

✧ Lead subtly, gently to the truth.

✧ Search for the student's good qualities,
    no matter how thoroughly covered.

✧ Once the student is aware of the problem,
    no need to nag.

The Unaccepted

He was unwanted
    shunned by his peers,
        untouchable—
            a leper.

His request, a simple
    "Sir, if you want to you can make me clean!"

The response of the concerned Teacher
    must have stunned the observers:

He "reached out and *touched him.*"
    He touched the untouchable!

    "I do want . . . Be clean."

He further directed the man
    to fulfill the prescription of the Law
    "to prove to everyone that you are now clean."

The cleansed man needed
    not only to know that he was healthy,
        but to regain acceptance by his family
            and his community.   Lk 5:12-16

And NOW
when we teach our unaccepted ones . . .

✧ Our unaccepted ones include
    . . . those with limited talents and intelligence,
    . . . the grubby,
    . . . the uncoordinated,
    . . . those shunned because of handicaps,
    . . . the unloved,
    . . . the in-group's outsiders.

✧ "Touch them" in the presence of their peers
... by recognizing the worth of their ideas,
... by seeking out their opinion and acting on it,
... by appointing them to jobs that indicate
your respect for their ability.

✧ Any student's self-acceptance hinges greatly
on the acceptance received
from both peers
and significant adults.

* * *   * * *   * * *

The Gifted

He had been studying the Teacher.

Nicodemus had thought profoundly enough
about the Teacher's message
to be filled with questions.
No surface information
could furnish answers;
no quick response could satisfy.

He was also on the verge
of breaking away from peer pressure.

He needed time
and privacy,
and individualized attention . . .
all needs of the gifted learner.

So, he approached the Teacher
in the privacy provided by darkness—"after class."

And the Teacher gave him time and undivided attention.
He answered questions
and expanded the lesson as much
as *this* mind could handle.   Jn 3:1-12

—

46

And NOW
when we teach our gifted ones . . .

✧ Be alert for the "after class" needs of students.

✧ Be conscious of eager students who,
  influenced by the need of acceptance
  by peers who are average,
  shy away from appearing interested in learning.

✧ Stretch a mind as far as it wants to expand.

✧ Know that
  the most important results of instruction
  are not evident at the close of a single lesson.

Jn 7:50; 19:39-42

* * *   * * *   * * *

The Crafty

Luke tells us quite a lot
    about Zacchaeus
        in the first few verses of Chapter 19.

He was rich,
    curious,
        short,
            inventive,
                agile—in that order.

Only his occupation
    would have made him suspect.

Tax collectors weren't known for honesty.
    Craftiness, yes.
    Honesty, no.

Zacchaeus must have felt important,
    since Jesus met his need to be recognized
        first by calling him by name,
        and then by inviting himself
            to be a guest
            in the flustered man's house.

It's interesting to note:
    it was the man's neighbors
        who pointed out his sinfulness,
    not the all–knowing Jesus.

And the addled Zacchaeus
    responded to the Teacher
        by announcing his sudden intention
        of splitting his belongings with the poor;
            and, just in case
            of some forgotten moment of deception,
        of repaying fourfold
            anybody he'd cheated.

A spur-of-the-moment decision
        to make restitution
        before being accused of dishonesty
            might indicate a troubled conscience.

And how did the Teacher respond?

He rejoiced at the conversion!
    No "It's about time, Zach!"
    No penance given;
        just rejoicing.

"Salvation has come to this house today;
    this man also is a descendant of Abraham.
        For the Son of Man came
            to seek and to save
                the lost."   Lk 19:1-10

And NOW
when we teach our crafty ones . . .

✧ All students need recognition—assurance that others
   are aware of their personal worth and dignity.

✧ Learn students' names as soon as possible.
   This says to each one: "You are important to me."

✧ Praise students for their improvement, their effort.
   Actual achievement will follow soon after.

✧ A thought:
   No mention is made in Scripture about how lasting
   Zacchaeus's conversion was.
       "Zacchaeus people" seem to be quick
       to admit mistakes and
       promise amendment
           —but perhaps, just as quick
           to forget the whole thing.

   Still, Jesus reached out, offering an opportunity,
       without scheduling a post-test.

   He believed in each student!

       * * *   * * *   * * *

The Shy

Nothing distinctive
    marked the woman's appearance.
Physically, she was weak
    from twelve years of hemorrhaging.
Financially, she was poor,
        having spent all she had
            in search of doctors and cures.

49

In desperation,
    she had joined the throng
        of believers
        and curiosity seekers
            who accompanied the Teacher,
            on the way to the sickbed
            of a little girl.

Only the woman's desire to be healed
    and her confidence in the power
        of the Teacher
            were strong.

In her timidity,
    she managed to edge her way
        close enough to touch the fringe of his cloak,
            and then slipped back into the crowd,
                as she became aware of a sense
                of physical strength
                and wholeness
                    surging through her body.

This model of shyness and fearfulness
    escaped the notice of everybody
        except Jesus,
            who turned instantly
                searching the crowd for her.

When the woman became aware of her discovery
    she stammered out what she had done.

Jesus respected her shyness.
    By keeping his response short,
        he did not prolong her moment
            in the spotlight.

He simply encouraged her,

    "Your faith has made you well."   Mk 5; 25-34; Lk 8:42-4

And NOW
when we teach our shy ones . . .

✧ Avoid limelight situations which tend to embarrass.

✧ Recognize that some students work best
in settings away from footlights and fanfare.

And every production depends upon
the writers and producers, the costume designers
and directors of lighting and stage sets—
whom the audience never sees.

The Persevering Searcher

When he first came to know her
her life was controlled by seven demons.
And he put her life back
into her own hands.   Lk 8:2

She chose to spend her time accompanying him
as he preached the Good News
through towns and villages.

The evangelists refer to her past
but spare her the embarrassment
of describing it.

They become specific when they list her
with the few women
who kept vigil with his mother
at the foot of his cross,   Jn 19:25
and before his newly sealed tomb
on that Sabbath eve.   Mk 15:47

51

Mary Magdalene
— distraught organizer of the Easter Morning grave visit,
    who remembered to bring spices to anoint him,
    but overlooked the detail
        about moving the stone   Mk 16:1-4
— woman with a single purpose:
    not to be separated
    from the source of her strength
    and her peace.

She was unbelievably persevering
  . . . despite the apparently superfluous message
    of the inconsequential angels
    who simply told her what she could see:
        "He is not here!"   Lk 24:6
  . . . despite the off-handed reception
    she received from his unbelieving
    and slow-moving disciples;
  . . . through the frantic search she started on her own
    to find him
  . . . through the agonizing tears of grief
    and another frustrating encounter with angels
    who only asked her questions
    rather than answer the only one that mattered:
        Where have they put him?
  . . . through the last encounter with the "gardener"!

And how does he treat her?

He commissions her
    to deliver the Good News of his Resurrection
    to his Twelve.

Another first!
  — a person with a past
    commissioned to herald the future:

        "Go to my brothers and tell them that
        I am returning to him
        who is my Father and their Father,
        my God and their God."   Jn 20:17–18

———

— a persevering woman
        sent to proclaim his message
        to the bewildered ones
           who would be his first bishops.

He isn't bothered by protocol.
He ignores tradition.

He commissions Mary
    — for who she is
    — for what she has become
    — for her ability to get things done
    — for the potential he sees in her.

The evangelists never mention her again.
No need to.

And NOW
when we teach our persevering ones . . .

✦ Do we appreciate those
    who won't let the question drop until they understand
        — or, finding them annoying,
           do we tease them into satisfaction
             with surface knowledge?

✦ Do we open new avenues of exploration
    for their inquisitive minds
        — or do we become aggravated
        at their restlessness
           when we offer them conformity with
             how we've always done it?

✦ Do we meet students where they are
        — or where we wish they were,
           or where last year's class was by now?

53

✧ Do we reward the leadership and creativity
    that take our students beyond
    what we are capable of,
      — or is there a greenish tint
      to our reluctant attempt
        to encourage critical thinking
        and independence?

    Jesus encouraged independence and leadership
      in all his students
        for he was leaving his message
          for future generations in their hands.
    And if our message *today* is still his,
      should we do less?

             * * *   * * *   * * *

The Obstinate

Knowing the hearts of people
    was a mark of the Master Teacher.

But, in spite of what he knew about Judas Iscariot,
    — a thief, a potential traitor,
      one who would take his own life —
        the Teacher chose him as one of the Twelve.

Why? What else did he see in Judas?
    What were his hopes for this one?

Every time the names
    of Jesus and Judas
      appear in the same few verses,
        what shines through
      is the never failing perseverance
    of the Master
      in giving repeated occasions
        for Judas to begin his growth in faith.

When Judas remarks on the wasted perfume
    and the missed chance of giving to the poor,
    Jesus simply defends the woman's action.   Jn 12:1-8

At the Last Supper,
    after washing the feet of Judas,
        Jesus says: "One of you is going to betray me,"
        providing enough time for Judas
        to rethink what he is about to do.

And Jesus protects his obstinate one's reputation
by covering for him.

    "Hurry and do what you must!"

    . . . leaving the others to wonder
        if Judas is being sent
            to get something else for supper
            or to give money to the poor.   Jn 13:2

Even in the garden, on Thursday night,
    Jesus responds with a question
        to his traitorous kiss and greeting:
            "Peace with be with you, Teacher,"
        — not a reprimand, but a question:

    "Is it with a kiss, Judas,
        that you betray the Son of Man?"
        And Jesus calls him "friend."

Obviously, Judas regretted his actions,
    but he'd never absorbed the lessons
        that Jesus repeated so many times.
        . . . Forgiveness…seventy times seven
        . . . Love of enemies
        . . . Turning the other cheek
        . . . "Love one another as I have loved you."
                Jn 13:1-30

And NOW
when we teach our obstinate ones . . .

✧ Never give up on these most needy of students.

✧ They're really desperate for all the opportunities
we can give them,
— even when they aren't aware
of how much they really need those chances.

✧ Patience must mark our dealings with them.

✧ We can never control
a student's motivations, decisions, or actions.

All we can do is offer
information,
our example,
and our prayer for the obstinate one.

✧ Perhaps Judas was included among the Twelve
to keep us aware that even the Master
couldn't teach somebody who didn't want to learn

. . . and to inspire us to keep on trying anyway.

PART THREE

SMALL GROUP INSTRUCTION:
HIS HOMEROOM

SMALL GROUP INSTRUCTION: HIS HOMEROOM

Fortunate are the teachers
    of the self-contained classroom,
        and those who have a homeroom.
Jesus, the Master Teacher, could say:
    "So did I!"

Possibly
    his contacts with the many individuals
    who remain unnamed by the evangelists
        were once-in-a-lifetime meetings;
    and those in the crowds,
        perhaps had few, if any, personal encounters
        with the Teacher.

In each instance
    Jesus was gentle
    or firm
        as the situation demanded.

With his Twelve
    it was an entirely different matter.
He was with them daily
    as a teacher is with a class.

Surely there must have been
    — good days
        and bad ones
    — occasions when the group was in high spirits
        and sometimes, low
    — times of seriousness
        and times of humor.

He was molding, guiding, forming them.

They were being prepared to continue his work,
    although they didn't seem to understand that
        until the last few days of their schooling.

So, they needed praise,
    encouragement,
        correction,
            challenges,
                empathy.

And he provided for all their needs.

The way he dealt with the variety among his Twelve
    in personality,
    in ability,
    and in the degree of cooperation
        gives any preK-12 teacher
        inspiration
        and direction.

        * * *   * * *   * * *

From the very beginning
    he set about
    imbedding the mark of his philosophy
        firmly in their hearts.

As early as Matthew's ninth chapter,
    he tried to instill in them
        his love of his mission.

    "There is a large harvest,
        but few workers to gather it in.

    Pray to the owner of the harvest
        that he will send out workers
            to gather in his harvest."   Mt 9:37-38

But he wasn't waiting around
    for somebody else to do the job.

He told Peter and the others:

    "We must go on
    to the other villages around here.
      I have to preach in them also,
      because that is why I came."   Mk 1:38-39

He went into great detail
    about what it meant
    to *belong* to this homeroom,
       — clear unmistakable directions
          for a challenging future
          if they chose to stay with him,
       — with no apologies
          for the difficulties they would entail.

And his students reached for the challenge
    because they saw a perfect example
    in the Teacher.   Mt 10:5-15

      * * *   * * *   * * *

During his three or so years with them
    he developed new concepts:
      . . . about not retaliating   Mt 5:38-42
      . . . about loving one's enemies,   Mt 5:43-48
      . . . about the new view of the Sabbath,   Mt 12:1-8
      . . . about a unique form of prayer.   Mt 6:9-13

He gave them ample opportunities
    to practice and apply those lessons
      under his close supervision.

He created a variety of learning experiences
    that they never forgot.

Consider what the Twelve must have learned when he

. . . sent them on surprising errands   Lk 19:28-36; 22:7-13
. . . posed problems to challenge   Jn 13:4-17
. . . warned them about evil influence   Mt 23:1-12
. . . puzzled them   Jn 20:3-10; Mk 4:34
. . . gave them advice   Lk 12:1-5
. . . corrected them   Jn 12:4-8; Mk 8:33
. . . grouped them, apparently without
      causing jealousy among them   Mk 5:37; 9:2; 14:33
. . . gave orders   Lk 9:1-6
. . . forced them to take a stand on issues   .Mk 8:27-30
. . . asked for their assistance, support   Mt 26:36-38
. . . defended them   Mt 12:1-8; Jn 18:7-9
. . . responded to their petitions   Lk 11:1-13
. . . scolded them   Mk 16:14
. . . teased them into learning   .Lk 24:13-35
. . . aroused their curiosity   Mk 13:1-6ff
. . . prepared them gently for a difficult situation   Jn 13:21-30
. . . gave them extra help
      with hard lessons   Lk 8:9-18; Mk 4:34
. . . introduced them to prayer by his example   Mk 1:35-38
. . . made them come to grips
      with what they believed   Lk 9:18-20
. . . expressed impatience with their slowness   Mk 8:14-21
. . . gave them a chance to save face   Jn 21:15-19
. . . affirmed them for going beyond
      what was taught   Mt 16:17
. . . took them on field trips always to strengthen their faith
      — to Cana for a wedding feast   Jn 2:1-12
      — on a walk to find a fig tree   Mk 11:12-14; 20-24
      — to Bethany for a resurrection   Jn 11:11-44
      — to Mount Tabor for a meeting   Mk 9:2-10

Not only did he explain his mission,
   he empowered the Twelve with his authority
     to do what he could do:
      "Drive out evil spirits
      and to heal every disease
       and every sickness."   Mt 10:1

He was mindful of a purpose of *all* teaching:

   to develop independence in the student.

       * * *   * * *   * * *

Jesus earned the respect and trust of the Twelve.
They obviously were in awe of him,
   but in their early attempts
     to use his healing power
     which he had shared with them,
        they weren't always successful.

It was evidently with great relief
   that the man
     whose son was possessed by an evil spirit
     saw Jesus.

Some of the Teacher's disciples
   had made an unsuccessful attempt
   to heal the troubled boy;
     and that had resulted
      in drawing a curious crowd
       to witness the argument that ensued
        between the frustrated disciples
        and the boy's disappointed father.

Jesus took command of the situation;
   and for the next eight verses
   Mark omits any reference
     to the disciples watching the scene intently
     from the sidelines.

63

Mark refers to them again
   "after Jesus had gone indoors."
Only then, did they ask him in private:

    "Why couldn't we drive the spirit out?"

They referred to the failure
   not *he.*
They felt comfortable
   and secure in his presence.
They knew he would not ridicule their efforts
   and their failure;
      he would simply give them
      further instruction:

    "Only prayer can drive this kind out,
      nothing else can."   Mk 9:14-28

     * * *   * * *   * * *

On another occasion
   the disciples had just heard Jesus
      — in one packed sentence —
   predict the destruction of the Temple:

    "Not a single stone will be left in its place;
    every one of them will be thrown down."   Mk 13:2

    For Peter, Andrew, James, and John,
      such an answer needed expansion;
      so they "came to him in private.
        Tell us when this will be."

His consistency of manner
   made them certain
      that they would be answered
     at length.
         And they were right.   Mk 13:5-37

His students were eager,
but not always sharp!

They had just witnessed some Pharisees
      attempting to entrap the Teacher;
         and perhaps, it had unnerved them a bit . . .
            They were too distracted to remember
         to pack enough lunch
           for the boat trip across the lake.

Then, they mistook
      his reminder about "yeast of Pharisees"
      to be a reprimand
         about their forgetfulness.

Embarrassment has a way
      of compounding troubles
         — and they were embarrassed.

And he must have been a bit edgy:

  "Don't you know or understand yet?
      Are your minds so dull?"

But he did a quick review
      reminding them of the bread-miracles
         they had recently witnessed.

         "How is it that you don't understand
           that I was not talking to you
           about bread?"

Matthew's verse twelve begins with
"*Then* the disciples understood."   Mt 16:5-12

      . . . Development: no response.
      . . . More development: misunderstanding.
      . . . Review and drill: *maybe* a little understanding.

It was that way when he taught.
Why should it be different for us?

—
65

He was able
    to create a wonderful rapport
        with his homeroom group.

He loved and respected them
    and they obviously knew that
    because *they returned that love and respect.*

Evidently they felt
    comfortable enough with him
    to speak in a very familiar fashion,
        without his taking it amiss.

* * *   * * *   * * *

They must have been wild in panic
    as the crashing waves
        began to drench them
        and fill their wind-whipped boat.

To add to their distress,
    the Teacher slept soundly in the stern,
    his head cushioned comfortably
        on a pillow!

But the awakening must have been a jolting one
    As, distraught, they shouted:
        "TEACHER, DON'T YOU CARE
        THAT WE ARE ABOUT TO DIE?"

He *"commanded"* the wind
    but he *"said"* to his disciples,
        probably in a tone that matched the ensuing calm:

        "Why are you frightened?
        Are you still without faith?"   Mk 4:35-41

* * *   * * *   * * *

They seemed to be protective of him:

. . . His disciples were good
    at reminding the Teacher
      of his usual schedule lest he forget.

    When the crowds began to assemble,
      Simon and the others spent time
      searching for him;
        and they found him
        in his lonely place of prayer.
They seemed to ignore
what he'd been doing and told him,
        "Everyone is looking for you."   Mk 1:35-36

. . . And after some stiff words
    to the Pharisees,
      the Teacher heard a friendly cautioning
      from his Twelve:
      "Do you know
        the Pharisees had their feelings hurt
      by what you said?"   Mt 15:12

. . . As crowds of people
    swarmed about him on the way
      to Jairus' house,
        he sensed the touch
        of someone in need of his healing power.

    "Who touched my clothes?" he asked.

    His disciples had the answer:
      "You see how the people are crowding you;
        Why do you ask who touched you?"

His response?

    "But Jesus kept looking around to see who had done it."
    — no rebuke for words that an insecure teacher
      might have considered
      rude or disrespectful.   Mk 5:29-32

. . . But once,
   when Simon protested
   his prediction of suffering and death,
      this apostle heard the teacher's rebuke. Mk 8:32-33

* * *   * * *   * * *
. . . .

Jesus concluded
   his disciples' brief education
   with a significant supper.

He reviewed the major concepts
   he had taught,
   he summarized his philosophy,
      and he designated the hallmark of his school:
         that his disciples have love for one another.

And NOW
when we teach our homeroom group . . .

✧ When there is mutual love and respect
      between teacher and students,
         openness can grow.
      Tone of voice, words,
                  even interpretation of motives
                  become funneled
                  through understanding and trust.

✧ But teachers who *expect* and *wait for*
         their students' respect without teaching it
            wait in vain.
   Students have a way of reflecting the respect
         given them by their teachers.

68

PART FOUR

JESUS AND LEARNING STYLES

JESUS AND LEARNING STYLES

In recent years, we have heard much about learning styles as if this were a brand-new concept. A meditative perusal of the Scriptures shows us that Jesus knew exactly how to adapt his teaching to his students' modes of learning. Visual, auditory, and kinesthetic learners found themselves absorbing lessons specifically designed for them.

* * *   * * *   * * *

Jesus and Auditory Learners

For some of his students,
   Jesus recognized that *hearing the message*
     was sufficient for them to grasp it.
For these, he left the application of that message
   in their hands.

He provided many auditory experiences.
   His Sermon on the Mount
     and all his parables were delivered orally,
   as were his many question/answer sessions.

Among his auditory learners were these:

> A teacher of the Law
   — heard the description
     of how to he was to treat his neighbor.   Lk 10:25-37

> Mary, sister of Martha and Lazarus,
   — sat at his feet, "listening to his teaching"
     and earned a complaint from her busy sister.

Lk 10:38-41

> ### The rich young man
> — engaged in a lengthy question/answer session
> that disappointed him.   Mt 19:16-23; Mk 10:17-21

> ### His homeroom group
> — requested an instruction on prayer
> and was rewarded
> with not only the Our Father
> but a parable encouraging them
> to pray it daily.   Lk 11: 1-13

> ### Simon the Pharisee and his dinner guests
> — heard a tailor-made parable about debtors
> as Jesus defended the gentle actions
> of a known sinner.   Lk 7:36-50

> ### His 72 disciples
> — received only oral instructions
> about just how they were to travel
> to spread the Good News.
> — On returning they reported their success,
> evidently the result
> of following those directions.   Lk 10:1-12, 17

> ### His Twelve
> — took part in a question/answer session
> that resembled an end-of-unit quiz.
>
> "Who do people say I am?"
> "Who do you say I am?"   Mk 8:27-30

But Simon Peter was well prepared.

* * *   * * *   * * *

Jesus and Visual Learners

The Master recognized the characteristics
    of those who learn best by seeing
        and observing demonstrations.

He made certain
    that his apostles would feel confident
        as he prepared them
        to heal and teach in his name.

He had a way of focusing his students' attention
    on the learning of the moment
        — often before he made them aware
        of what they were to observe.

He pointed out a fig tree
    both before and after
    it had no fruit to offer him.   Mk 11:12-14; 20-24

He took three disciples up a mountain
    to see him transfigured
    and witness an unforgettable meeting
    involving himself, Moses, and Elijah.   Mk 9: 2-10

Watching people dropping their Temple tax
into the treasury, he noticed her.
    The widow's two copper coins and her motive
    were perfect for a lesson
    on generous giving.
So he called his disciples over and said . . ."   Mk 12: 41-44

He stood a child before them
and taught them about simplicity and innocence
    and the dignity of children.   Mt 18:2-4

He directed,
    "Look at the birds," and
    "Look how the wild flowers grow,"
to teach about God's tender care for us.   Mt 6:26, 28

73

To answer the Pharisees' trick question about taxes,
he had them show him a coin and asked
whose face and name were on it.   Mt 22:17-21

* * *   * * *   * * *

Jesus and Kinesthetic Learners

It appears that Jesus was especially aware
of the need for his students
to be *doing* something
in order to learn.

He thoughtfully arranged activities
that would make his lessons come to life.

Peter was instructed
— to *catch* a fish, *open* its mouth, and *pay* the tax.   Mt 17:27
— to *"Bring* some of the fish you have just *caught."*   Jn 21:10
— to *"Come!"* and join the Master
for a *walk* on the water.   Mt 14:28-39

Moneychangers in the Temple heard the Teacher's shout!
They burst into action at his command,
chasing animals as they fled their broken crates
and cages
scrambling around and under tables,
between overturned chairs and benches,
snatching coins that rolled in all directions. Jn 2:13-16

They must have recalled this scene many times
— as often as they saw the Teacher
in the marketplace and in the Temple.

His apostles were very bodily engaged
— as they *searched* for available food
and *distributed* the few loaves and fishes
to thousands of hungry followers
— and as they *piled up* the leftovers
in twelve baskets.   Mt 14:13-21

**And NOW
when we adapt to our students'
learning styles . . .**

✧ The monotonous lecture/note-taking method
    may have been highly respected
        when it was the primary way to deliver learning
           in pre-technology days.

      But that was then. ...This Is Now!
    Today lecturing is *one* way, not *the* way of teaching.

✧ Close observation of our students as they learn
      is the key to discovering how best to teach them.

✧ Our preferred choice of teaching may need
      to bend and stretch
      in order to accommodate each one's
        best learning style.

✧ The older the students are,
      the more variety can be built
        into their learning activities.

Be aware of the auditory learners.

    ✧ They need to *hear*
      oral directions and explanations.

    ✧ They need to *participate* in discussions
        with the teacher
        and their classmates.

    ✧ They are easily distracted
      by extraneous sound,
        even soft music during intellectual tasks.

75

Be aware of the visual learners.

✧ They need to *see, read, observe* demonstrations.

✧ They need to *see* new words and ideas
written on Smartboards
as explanations are given orally.

✧ They are easily distracted
by extraneous visuals
and cluttered surroundings.

Be aware of the kinesthetic learners.

✧ It seems that their needs are mostly ignored
at middle grade and junior high levels.
By high school and college,
their needs are often forgotten altogether.

But their needs must be met at *all* learning levels

✧ They need to handle manipulatives
as they learn math and science.

✧ They learn through writing, drawing,
and creating models of what they study.

✧ They learn through movement, rhythm, song,
and dance
— and by creating their own.

✧ They learn through skits, plays, and role playing.

✧ They learn by manipulating computers and iPads
and by playing video games.

PART FIVE

THE MASTER TEACHER'S CURRICULUM

THE MASTER TEACHER'S CURRICULUM

We have looked at how the Master adapted his teaching to the needs of large and small groups and of individuals, and to students' learning styles. But what was the content of his instruction?

* * *   * * *   * * *

A graduate of the Master's school
could expect to learn concepts totally foreign
to the religious beliefs of that time.

In the beginning class,
(usually referred to as the Sermon on the Mount),
although he made no mention of objectives
or essential questions and enduring learning,
he made his expectations of student performance
perfectly clear.

His expectations were high—
cloud-piercingly high.
He offered no shortcuts.
He just elaborated on the goals,
set the example by modeling the whole thing,
and simply expected his students to learn.

His graduates were to be
... lights on lamp stands   Lk 11:33-36
... salt that adds flavor   Mt 5:13
... models of goodness.   Mt 5:16

All his students were to go beyond the law
that forbade murder...
They were to avoid even anger!   Mt 5:21-22

They were to be pure of heart,
    known for clean living,
    and so trustworthy,
        that oaths would be unnecessary.   Mt 5:33-36

They were to be generous with possessions,   Mk 10:21
    compassionate,
    and astoundingly patient
    and gentle enough
        to turn the other cheek.   Mt 5:39

They were to accept others
    without passing judgment on them.   Mt 7:1

They were to be known for their love
    of their brothers
        and strangers,
            and even enemies.   Jn 13:35

They were to forgive as generously
    as God had forgiven them.   Mt 6:14

They were to be unobtrusive as they worshipped
    and did their deeds of mercy,
    which they evidently were expected to
        do lots of.   Mt 6:5

They were to be cheerful when they fasted
    and prefer long-lasting spiritual treasures
        over material wealth.   Mt 6:16-18

They were to live simply,
    and trust God to know all their needs
        and to provide for them.

They were to stop worrying
    and use the wildflowers
        and sparrows
    to remind them
        of God's provident care.   Mt 6:26

And, as if this weren't enough,
> they were to treat others as they'd like to be treated
> — and keep an eye out for false teachers
> > who came in everyday disguises
> > to distract and mislead them.

Of course, they'd need a great deal of help living this way.
So, they were to remember to pray to the Father
> — even daily,
> > for all the strength they'd need
> > > to reach the goals.   Mt 6:9-13

Somebody surely must have asked the usual
> "and what if we do all these things,
> > what do we get?"

No homework passes, M & M treats, or pizza parties—
> just the assurance that you will be
> > as wise as the person who builds a house safely,
> > high up on rock
> > > instead of on sand.

And NOW
what can 21st century teachers
learn from all this? . . .

✧ First, we need to examine ourselves to find out
> just how much of this we are living.
> > We can't teach believable lessons
> > > if we don't demonstrate our faith in the content
> > > of what we teach.

✧ However,
> we can't postpone teaching all these things
> until we're perfect examples of them.
> > We would never be ready to teach!

✧ Considering all the second chances
  the Master showered about
  as he guided his students,
    his perfection will have to fill
      the many gaps there are
        between what we are
        and what we ought to be.

That being said, we can move
  to *ways of teaching* his curriculum.

✧ PreK–12 teachers of all subjects
    can take every opportunity
    to use all literary genres
      that feature themes, characters, and plots
      that exemplify the Master Teacher's lessons,
        and some that show the consequences
        of ignoring his message.

✧ Those who teach social studies
      will find endless examples
    of individuals, groups, and nations
        that created either positive or negative
        events that can be used to enrich a lesson.

✧ Current newspapers and magazines
    will update those events.

✧ Music, painting, dance, drama, and all the fine arts
      have the potential of humanizing
      those who participate in them.

✧ Those who teach science, health, and physical education
      have plenty of opportunities to inspire students
        with awe as they consider the beauty of creation
        and the loving Creator of it all.

✧ The application of the Master Teacher's curriculum
      will depend upon how faithfully today's teachers
        deliver his Good News.

Life-Changing Lessons

A graduate of the Master's school
would have spent extra time concentrating on
life-changing lessons.

Those lessons that Jesus wanted to instill
were taught again and again
with all the variety he could muster.

He used this system for concepts he valued most.

Forgiveness of Sins

Although they'd seen him forgive the sins
of the paralyzed man   Lk 5:20
and the woman
with the alabaster perfume jar   Lk 7:36-39

and they'd heard him *preach* forgiveness
— even if the brothers came
seven times in one day to apologize   Lk 17:3
— even if Peter's hypothetical brother
offended him another seven times.   Mt 18 21-22

How unprepared they were
for his own example of forgiveness . . .

"Forgive them, Father!
They don't know what they are doing."   Lk 23:34

How astounded to hear him
empower them to continue his forgiving . . .

"Receive the Holy Spirit,
If you forgive men's sins
they are forgiven."   Jn 20:22-23

* * *   * * *   * * *
· · · ·   · · · ·   · · · ·

Earthly Riches

They had seen him *poor in things*,
yet rich in generosity with his time,
and his gift of miracles.

They probably weren't very surprised
to hear him direct them:

"So don't be all upset, always concerned
about what you will eat and drink . . . .

Instead, be concerned with his Kingdom
and he will provide you with these things." Lk 12:29-31

* * *   * * *   * * *

Prayer

Early in the disciples' education
they evidently missed the point entirely.

Though they were in awe of the teacher's habit
of seeking out lonely places   Lk 5:16
in the only uninterrupted time he had
— from late at night
through the early morning hours—
they didn't hesitate
to charge in to announce visitors.   Mk 1:35

Perhaps they'd learned
to take his prayer for granted,
since "on the Sabbath day
he went *as usual* to the synagogue."   Lk 4:16

They gradually must have become aware
of the necessity of prayer
as they observed
the value he placed upon it.

His prayer seemed to be in proportion
    to events he prayed about
        — forty days of it
            before beginning his public teaching
                Mt 4:2; Mk 1:12-13; Lk 4:1-13
        — a night of it
            before he chose his disciples.   Lk 6:12-16

They must have been surprised to hear him
        — direct them to pray for their persecutors   Mt 5:44-45
        — insist that they pray
            in the privacy of their own room
            and in few words.   Mt 6:5-13
        — encourage them to imitate
            the persistent widow and the tax collector
        — tell them to pray always
            and never get discouraged.   Lk 18:1
        — encourage them to gather in little groups
            for prayers.
                Mt 18:19-20

They must have noted
the powerful answers to his prayer
        — after his baptism   Lk 3:21-22
        — when Lazarus walked out of his tomb   Jn 11:41-44
        — when Peter, James, and John
            went up a mountain with him to pray
            and discovered Moses and Elijah.   Lk 9:28-36

And one time when he finished praying,
        they had seen enough, been inspired enough
        to want to know how to pray.
        And he taught them his prayer,
        the Our Father.   Lk 11:1-13

His final instruction was again his example:
        praying to the Father for the eleven of them
            at the Last Supper
            while they watched intently,
                not really understanding.   Jn 17:1-26

85

And then later, praying in the garden for himself
   while instead of praying as he asked,
      they slept.
                        Mt 26:36-41; Mk 14:32-40; Lk 22:39-46

* * *   * * *   * * *

Respect for Every Person's Dignity

He had compassion on the tax collectors
and other outcasts who came to hear him.
     They saw themselves in his parables
        about the lost son,
           sheep, and coins.   Lk 15:1-32

They must have been a little flattered
     as they sheepishly heard
     their techniques described
        in the shrewd manager's dealings.   Lk 5:27-32

But they knew he respected them.
     Hadn't he already chosen one of them
     as his disciple?

     Hadn't they attended the fine banquet
     Levi gave to celebrate his calling
        where other tax collectors were guests? Lk 5:27-32

And the same respect he'd shown
to each questionable character:
     — the woman caught in adultery   Jn 8:1-11
     — the tree-climbing tax collector   Lk 19:1-10
     — the woman possessed of seven demons   Lk 8:2

they saw again as he welcomed the thief
     to join him in paradise.   Lk 23:43

     He lived his message as he taught it.

—

And NOW
when we teach our life-changing
lessons . . .

Layered teaching still works.
Let our students see the lesson
in our attitudes and actions
before they hear what they're to be learning.

✧ *Awareness digs the hole for the foundation.*
No value in testing at this point;
only the most perceptive students
may have grasped the lesson.
For students to absorb a life-changing idea, they need
— to examine it in many ways,
— to be immersed in it,
— to practice it,
— and to have opportunities
to live it and see it lived.

✧ **Instruction erects the scaffolding.**
Not much value in testing at this point.
Only some students may have learned the lesson,
with varying degrees of accuracy.
Total acceptance is usually gradual,
the slight change, imperceptible.
Even the students aren't aware
of how much they've actually learned,
until and unless the lesson is challenged,
sometimes years after the initial learning.

✧ **Living the lesson brings the edifice to completion.**
By the time the students are ready for testing,
the period of learning may be months,
even decades in the past—
long after the students have forgotten
the teacher's carefully prepared lessons
and probably, even the teacher.

PART SIX

STUDENT INVOLVEMENT IN LEARNING

STUDENT INVOLVEMENT IN LEARNING

Learning *happens* through experience, study, or by being taught. Probably students' memories of learning are the most vivid if those recollections involved active participation in the event.

Jesus was truly a master in creating unique lessons that involved his students' minds and hands.

* * *   * * *   * * *

One impressive lesson
        made such an impact on the apostles
        that all four evangelists
                contribute to the telling of it.

It must have lasted the better part of a day;
        and it's possible to find
        the integration of at least eight techniques
                that would pass the test
        of *master teaching*.
                Mt 14:13-21; Mk 6:30-44; Lk 9:10-17; Jn 6:1-13

A long busy day of preaching
        was coming to an end.
The Teacher and his disciples
        hadn't had a moment to themselves,
                not even to eat.

Jesus had just suggested
        that they stop and rest for a while.
He was concerned
        about the welfare of his apostles,
        his student teachers.

But the crowds had followed them,
    and he was concerned about them, too.

The disciples,
    evidently accustomed to
    having their opinions respected, quickly suggested
        that the crowds be dispersed
            to give them a chance to buy food.   Mt 14:15

His answer must have stunned them:

    "They don't have to leave.
    You yourselves
        give them something to eat."   Mt 14:16

Jesus never missed an opportunity
    to prepare his apostles
    for their eventual assignment:
        of continuing his mission.

Too bad John didn't describe
    the expression in the Teacher's eyes
    when he said to Philip:

    "Where can we buy enough food
    to feed all these people?"   Jn 6:5

    Those eyes must have revealed
        at least some degree of teasing since
        he said this to test Philip.
        He actually already knew
            what he was going to do.   Jn 6:6

It was a little early for testing,
    insufficient time
    to have mastered
        the essentials of the lessons;
    but maybe Philip had given evidence
        of being quicker than others.

Obviously not.
Philip was still
on a beginner's level in discipleship,
although better at math.
He could see at a glance that
200 silver coins worth of bread wouldn't be enough.

Peter's brother, Andrew
who seemed to be an approachable man,
was in the habit of bringing people to Jesus:
first, his brother, Peter,   Jn 1:40-42
and later, some Greeks.   Jn12:20-22
And this time, he noticed a youngster
with five loaves and a couple of fish
and pointed him out to Jesus.   Jn 6:9

Satisfied that his apostles
were trying their best
to solve the problem,
using their own ingenuity and ability,
he gave them assistance   Jn 6:10-13
. . . in organizing:

"Make the people sit down in rows,
in groups of one hundred and groups of fifty."
("There was a lot of grass there"
for the first parish picnic.)

. . . in doing *only* what they could not do.
— He took the bread and fish
that they had produced.
— He thanked God for them
and broke them.

. . . in returning the ownership of the feast
back to his students.
— *They* distributed the food.
— *They* collected the leftovers.

And the apostles were astounded
by what they were able to do . . . with him.

93

And NOW
when we involve our students . . .

✧ Are we more concerned about our students' needs
  or about our own?

✧ Do we give them sufficient time and opportunity
    to try to solve problems
      before we offer some help
      — and then keep the assistance
        to a minimum?

✧ Are we satisfied to take a sideline seat
    while our students demonstrate their knowledge?

✧ Do we instill pride in our students
    by using what they contribute
      to their own learning?

✧ Do we keep our organization simple enough
    to permit our students
      to take command of their own learning?

* * *   * * *   * * *

Teamwork

Collaboration marked the very outset of his mission.
    Jesus and John the Baptist worked as a team,
      — with John beginning the mission
        and Jesus completing it.
      — with John encouraging his followers
          to transfer their allegiance from him
            to the Lamb of God.
        And this was done without a trace
        of selfishness
            or jealousy.

94

The concept of *team*
had been with the Teacher for a long time.

Even before there was a universe,
there was *the team*:
Father, Son, and Spirit

"The Son can do nothing on his own;
he does only what he sees
his Father doing."   Jn 5:19-47

"Then Jesus returned to Galilee
and the power of the Holy Spirit
was with him."   Lk 4:14

   * * *   * * *   * * *

At the beginning of his public teaching,
Jesus didn't select an administrative assistant.
He chose *a team of twelve*
and appointed Peter as group leader;
he obviously intended that his mission
would involve participation.   Mk 3:13-19

Jesus designed a support system for his team.

After preparing them thoroughly for the mission,
he sent them out
two-by-two,
providing them with companionship
and encouragement
as they spread the Good News.   Mk 6:7-12

The Twelve must have come to know one another
since Jesus often dealt with them as a group
and sub-groups.

95

Among the times he sent them
    in pairs or small groups
    to accomplish goals are these:
      — securing a colt for his entry
        into Jerusalem   Lk 19:28-36
      — preparing for his Last Supper.   Lk 22:7-13

         * * *   * * *   * * *

The Teacher frequently provided his students
    with opportunities for taking responsibility
    in completing tasks.

The newly-cleansed leper,
        in the midst of celebrating his cleansing
        realized that there was more to do
          besides celebrating.
He heard the directions:
      Go to the priest, be examined.
        And keep it a secret!   Mk 1:40

At the home of Simon the Pharisee,
      Jesus told the sinful woman,

      "Your faith has saved you; go in peace."   Lk 7:50

After ridding a man of demons,
      Jesus said to him:

      "Go back home and tell
        what God has done for you."   Lk 8:3

As the risen Jesus cooked breakfast on the beach,
   he told the seven disciples to bring some of the fish
      they just caught
and added their fish to the meal.   Jn 21:9–10

And NOW
when we group our students . . .

✧ Pairing or grouping students for learning projects
    can do wonders in creating an atmosphere
    of respect and cooperation in the classroom,
    as well as preparing young people
        for their adult lives
        as marriage partners
        and business teams.

✧ Learning games hold the attention of younger students
    while important concepts are reinforced.

-- Occasionally, before answering a question,
        the students could share their thoughts
        with a buddy or two,
            and then respond with the team's thoughts.

✧ The lessons they learn from such arrangements include
     — working together to achieve goals
     — respecting the talents and ideas of others
     — seeking and giving advice
     — listening and speaking courteously.

PART SEVEN

EDUCATIONAL TIPS FROM THE MASTER

EDUCATIONAL TIPS FROM THE MASTER

No how-to book for teachers is complete without a section on miscellaneous topics that are too scattered, and independently too insignificant to merit a whole chapter on each one. But every teacher recognizes the significance of the insignificant in dealing with students, equipment, and organization. In teaching, it's hard to find the insignificant. So, these topics are listed alphabetically to eliminate the need of listing them in the order of importance.

* * *   * * *   * * *

Children

Jesus apparently never provided any special classes
     to teach children his message.

He blessed them;
he put one in the midst
     of his ambitious apostles,
and he referred to them often enough
     to give a good indication
          of his attitude toward them.

As his apostles sheepishly looked
     at the child he had place in front of them,
          the Teacher spoke very forcefully:

"Unless you change and become like children
You will never enter the Kingdom of heaven.
The greatest in the Kingdom of heaven
     is one who humbles himself
     and becomes like this child.

And whoever welcomes in my name
    one such child as this,
                welcomes me."   Mt 18:2-4

            * * *   * * *   * * *

Jesus is recorded as being angry twice:
    once with the Temple moneychangers,
    and once with his disciples
        as they scolded the people
            who brought their children
            (Luke calls them "babies")
            for his blessing.

He spoke to the disciples:

"Let the children come to me, and do not stop them,
        because the Kingdom of God
        belongs to such as these."   Mk 10:14-16

But he blessed the children:
        "He took the children in his arms,
        and placed his hands on each of them
        and blessed them."

Matthew adds another insight
    into the Teacher's attitude toward children:

"See that you don't despise any of these little ones.
        Their angels in heaven, I tell you,
        are always in the presence
            of my Father in Heaven."   Mt 18:10

His view about those
    who would cause little ones to lose faith in him
        should make all teachers think seriously
        about their personal example,
        as well as how positively they deliver his message
        to children and young people.

Correcting Students

A significant part of teaching
   is correcting students.
Jesus used several techniques
   to accomplish this task.

— He *told a story*
   about the first and last places
     to correct some proud students.   Lk 14:7-14

— He *gave a warning*
   to the overly-confident Peter:
    "I tell you that before the rooster crows . . ."
                                 Mt 26:34

— A *look of reproof*
   was enough to make Peter remember
   the warning he had ignored earlier.
    "The Lord turned around
    and looked straight at Peter
     and Peter remembered."   Lk 22:61-62

— He gave a *sharp command* to Peter:
    "Put your sword back in its place!"   Jn 18:11

       * * *   * * *   * * *

It seems that the only times
   he used insulting, harsh words
   and dramatic, angry actions
     were when he was dealing
     with hearts hardened with years
      of adult choices
       of hypocrisy and greed,
       of pride and selfishness
        — the Scribes, the Pharisees,
        the moneychangers.

And NOW
when we correct our students . . .

❖ For those of us
    who deal with children,
        youth, and young adults,
    this manner of correction
        — insulting, harsh words
        and dramatic, angry actions —
    is totally out of place.

❖ Our students may be
    awkward, thoughtless, inconsiderate,
    clumsy, annoying, aggravating,
        and even obnoxious at times.

If they appear to be hardened,
    maybe we ought to look at the adult influences
    in their lives . . .
        — adult-produced films and television programs
        — adult-produced books and magazines
        — adult example all around them.

❖ *When we correct our students,*
        the gentle,
            forgiving,
                loving methods
        of the Master
            should be evident.

Behavior can be changed by
        simply calling a name or saying "No"
        shaking our head
        holding a private talk that begins,
            "I'm concerned about you."

Avoid the techniques Jesus used
        for hardened adults.

Directions

Directions

Universally, teachers fret
    over the inability of students
      to follow directions.
Some thirty years
      after his directions were given and followed,
        three of the evangelists
        were able to record them.

Excellent record!

Maybe the clarity did it:
    "Go to the village there ahead of you:
        as you go in you will find a colt tied up
          that has never been ridden.
      Untie it and bring it here.
      If someone asks you "Why are you untying it?"
      Tell him "the Master needs it."   Lk 19:31

    "And they went on their way and found everything
        just as Jesus had told them."

He was just as precise
    in his directions about the Passover meal,
        when Peter and John asked him:
        "Where do you want us to get it ready?"

Instead of answering with an address,
    Jesus told them they would see
      and should follow a man doing "women's work,"
        carrying a water jar.   Lk 22:10-13

In those prefeminist times,
    such a man
    probably would have been quite conspicuous!
And as usual they "found everything
    just as Jesus had told them."

          * * *   * * *   * * *

Earlier he had been just as explicit
    in his directions
  when he organized the Twelve
    for their first teaching experience.

He was very exact
    in listing everything
    they shouldn't take on the journey,
      things they'd expect
        an itinerant t teacher to pack:
          bread, bag, extra shirt, money,
            shoes, a walking stick.
Mt 10:9-10; Lk 9:3

However, in Mark's Gospel,
Jesus allowed the walking stick and sandals.   Mk 6:8-9

But Mark hadn't been there
    when the directions were given;
      he simply recorded
        what Peter remembered about the occasion.

So much for expecting exact directions
    to be repeated accurately.
      by a student
      for latecomers!

        * * *   * * *   * * *

Even in his miracle-working he was very definite:
    "Stretch out your hand."   Mt 12:13
    "Get up, pick up your mat and go home."   Mk 2:11
    "Go and let the priests examine you."   Lk 17:14

And the directions were always followed
    with exciting and astounding results.
It seems
    that the only times
    people ignored his directions
        were when the newly-cured were warned
        to tell no one what had happened.

And NOW
when we give directions . . .

✧ Directions need to be clear, to the point.

✧ Maybe we need to rethink
   the importance of the directions we give.
      How much is really necessary
      to achieve the major goal of the lesson?

✧ Do our students tend to get
   so entangled in the minutia of trifling, detailed directions
   and irrelevant rules of procedure
      that they lose sight of the learning before them?

Humor

Humor –
   quiet, gentle,
   sometimes seemingly tongue-in-cheek,
      but it was there.
Some scenes bring a smile
   as we read the details
      recorded so perceptively by the evangelists.

* * *   * * *   * * *

He made his disciples get into the boat
   and waved them off.
Then he dispersed the crowd
   and prayed into the night.

Before dawn, from the shore
   he saw that they were having a tough time
   rowing against the wind.
So he came to them walking on the water!   Mt 14:22-26

108

With more loyalty than information
Peter firmly assured the Temple tax collector
that the Teacher paid the required tax.

When Peter entered the house,
before he could open his mouth,
Jesus began speaking about taxes.

Then Jesus sent his prized fisherman
fishing for enough tax money
for both of them.   Mt 17:24-27

And NOW
when we use humor . . .

✧ Humor has a way of relaxing students
and aiding digestion of ideas
as well as lunch.

✧ Like salt and scarlet,
humor adds necessary flavor and color to learning,
if used in proper amounts.

✧ An occasional turn of words
or a look strategically timed
can bring a chuckle,
a shift of posture,
and encourage alertness
in our students.

While they're waiting for the next light moment,
some powerful lessons can be inserted.

✧ Humor should be light and free
– never at the expense
of a student's feelings.

109

Learning Settings

"I can't teach near the music room."
"I'd prefer a smaller room at the east end
of the old wing."
"It's useless to try to teach anything
. . . after Easter
. . . after two in the afternoon
. . . with more than twenty-three in a class."

We are so conscious
of when and where
we can or can't teach.
We do our best
when the place and the time are perfect.

Maybe we should glance at the settings
when Jesus did his best.

To cite a few . . .

— He explained the Beatitudes
sitting on a hillside,
surrounded by thousands.   Mt 5:1-12

— He taught at the lakeside
until he felt too crowded.

Then he moved to a boat
to create a bit of distance,
and so that his voice, by passing over water,
would be magnified.

From the boat, he taught the people
standing in the wet sand,
listening to the parables
he would explain later to his Twelve.   Mt 13:1-2

— He taught with just as much authority
    in the house of a tax collector,
    as he did in the synagogue.   Mt 9:10-13; Mk 1:21-22

— He taught in the towns   Mt 11:1
    and in lonely places,   Mk 1:45
      in a wheat field
         while his disciples snacked,   Mt 12:1-8
    and on the water
         while Peter sank.   Mt 14:28-33

— He taught in the Temple,
    surrounded by goats and doves
        and moneychangers.   Jn 2:13-20

— He taught at a wedding reception
    after the guests
    had depleted the refreshments.   Jn 2:1-12

— He taught at the grave of a dear friend   Jn 11:37-44
    and at the home of an enemy.   Lk 11:36-52

— The Upper Room was the center
    of some of his most intense instruction
      with his homeroom group,
        both before and after
        his resurrection.   Jn 13-17; 20:19-29

— He taught Nicodemus late at night,   Jn 3:1-20
    and Mary Magdalene as sunlight
      first touched his temporary tomb.   Jn 20:11-18

Even on the cross, he taught
    — as he was laying down his life
      for all those who would ever learn from him,
      and for those who wouldn't.
        Lk 23:34; 39-43; Jn 19:26-30

His best time
     seemed to have been
          all the time;
the best place,
          any place.

And NOW
about our learning settings . . .

✧ Perhaps the difference
     between his best setting and ours
          is the *view of the mission.*

✧ He knew that each moment
          would be the *only* moment
          for some student.

✧ He taught with an urgency
          because he had no more
               than three short years
     to accomplish his task.

     So, every moment
          in every setting
               became
     a teaching moment.

✧ And is it not the same with us?

          — Only we usually have only one year
          with a group of students.

          — Ought not our teaching
               reflect that same urgency?
               that same dynamism?

Member of a Staff

He worked well in departmentalized settings.
    John the Baptist had taught
        the readiness class in Christian Living.

Although Jesus took the beginners
and the advanced groups,
    he held in highest esteem
    the person of John and his work.

Jesus' words to the Baptist's disciples
    certainly must have given John
        a sense of worth and accomplishment,
        and given his message
            credibility in the minds of his disciples.

    "Remember this!
        John the Baptist is greater than
            any man who has ever lived."   Mt 11:7-15

And NOW
when referring to last year's teacher . . .

✧ Our students' previous teachers deserve our respect.
    If OUR message is to produce growth,
    it must be seen by our students
        as worthwhile knowledge
          to add to
what they have already acquired from former teachers.

✧ Teamwork among our faculty and staff
    who respect one another
will make a positive contribution
    to our students' education.

Multimedia

Though Jesus never prepared a PowerPoint presentation,
    it's likely that he had a say
    in his own birth announcement,
        — that spectacular use of media
           when the Father chose lights and singing angels
                to invite the shepherds;
                and for the Wise Men, a star.

For teaching aids,
    Jesus made the best use
        of available objects,
        produced at the most strategic moment.

He wasn't limited
    to props he could list
    on a requisition blank
        and submit by 2:15 p.m.
        on Tuesday.

He needed something
    a bit dramatic
        to build up the disciples'
           trust in him.
And a storm was the perfect teaching tool.   Mk 4:35-41

Sometimes a touch of drama does the same for us.

                      ★ ★ ★   ★ ★ ★   ★ ★ ★

He simply used
    — water,
        plain water and some nearby jars
           to begin to establish
           his credibility as Teacher.
    — and some available bread and fish
        to teach a lesson on caring.   Jn 2:1-12; 6:1-15

And as they were leaving the Temple
his disciples called his attention
to the building and its wonderful stones;
and he taught them a second lesson.
about what the future would hold.   Mk 12:41-44; 13:1-2

The Teacher met the man born blind
somewhere along the dusty road,
— hardly a place to find sophisticated equipment
and learning aids.
But he managed to make
a little healing mud
from his own spittle and the dust;
and taught his disciples
a lesson about the Light of the World.   Jn 9:6-7

A budget-of-nothing can produce creative adaptations.

He borrowed 2000 pigs
to rid a man of some demons.   Mk 5:1-19

The ground and his finger
substituted for a blackboard and chalk
or a whiteboard and markers.
Primitive, but effective
in clearing the area of some troublemakers.   Jn 8:1-11

A towel and a washbasin of water
were all he needed
to teach the Twelve an attitude of service.

"I have set an example for you. .. . .
How happy you will be
if you put it into practice."   Jn 13:4-17

Although he made use of many objects,
mostly, he used the touch of his hand
and gentle encouraging words
to heal the diseases of bodies and souls.

115

And NOW
when we select our teaching aids . . .

✧ In this time of catalogues of technological devices,
   maybe his message is:
      Effective use of a little
      can result in tremendous learning.

✧ The Teacher started by setting the GOAL of the lesson,
   then he selected his aids—never the reverse order.

Parent-Teacher Conference

In a moment of parental pride
      (or possibly at the suggestion of her sons),
         Mrs. Zebedee approached Jesus
         in the one recorded parent-teacher conference.

Salome was polite about it,
      bowing before the Teacher,
      and she wasn't the least bit hesitant
         in answering his: "What do you want?"

"*Promise* that these two sons of mine
      will sit at your right and your left
         when you are King."
Promise . . . A strong first word;
      and not for only one son,
         — but for both of them!

Jesus didn't answer *her*, he answered *them*.
He addressed his remarks to the students
      in the presence of the mother.

   "You don't know what you are asking for.
   Can you drink the cup that I am about to drink?" Mt 20:20-28

116

Salome

And NOW
at our parent-teacher conferences . . .

✧ Include the child with the parent at the conference.
Perhaps this technique
would put the focus on the trouble spot,
especially when stories
tend to develop many extra facets
and shades of meaning,
as they get retold in different settings
in the presence of different people.

Planning

Obviously, complex lessons
take more advanced planning
than simpler ones.

The Teacher had a way
of creating outstanding learning experiences.
The dramatic multiplication of loaves and fishes
and the generation of an instant storm to calm,
inspired wonder
and fanned the spark of faith
within his apostles.

         ★ ★ ★   ★ ★ ★   ★ ★ ★

In one instance
Jesus deliberately waited for days
before he responded to the summons
to visit his sick friend, Lazarus.

The Teacher had planned ahead
For the *most effective* of lessons.   Jn 11:1-44

On another occasion...
Jesus had begun his preparation
for a strategic lesson
probably *before his own birth*!
The Teacher and his followers
happened upon a blind man along the way;
and, in passing, the disciples inquired
about the cause of the blindness.
Was it the man's sinfulness or his parents'?

Jesus told them plainly
that nobody's sin had anything to do
with the man's condition.
But the fourth and fifth words of his next sentence
revealed some spectacular long-range planning.

"He is blind *so that* God's power might
be seen at work in him."   Jn 9:1-7

How's that for preparing for a lesson!

And NOW
when we plan . . .

✧ The teacher's attitude toward the real goal of the lesson
will determine how much time and effort
will go into the preparation for it.

✧ Although many effective lessons can be taught
and learned in spontaneous settings,
we can't depend on spontaneity
to provide for all lessons.
—If we don't make a conscious effort
to plan strategically and well in advance,
we're likely to limit our students' opportunities
to incidental learning.

September–June

In the "September" of his teaching,
    Jesus did much demonstrating
    and explaining,
        while his disciples were observing
            and asking questions.

By the "end of the first semester"
    his disciples were assisting him,
    — being sent *to use his power*
      in his name.

And during his last six weeks with them,
    he adjusted his methods again
    to meet their needs.

At the Last Supper
    he prayed *with them*
  and *for them.*
      He reviewed the highlights
        of all his teachings for them.
      He gave them final directions
      and prepared them
      to receive their next Teacher:

"The Helper, the Holy Spirit whom the Father
    will send in my name."   Jn 14:26

Then he put them through
    the most rigorous final examination
      from Thursday night
    until early Sunday morning,
      testing all they'd been taught by him.
And the testing results
    were enough to discourage any teacher!
    — One apparently failed.
    — And of the other eleven,
      all but one were too afraid
      to be present for the exam!

But testing only indicates how much more work
the teacher needs to do.

So, just look at the forty-day remediation
he provided before returning to his Father:
Faith must have been strengthened
and deepened;
hope, resurrected
with each of his encouraging appearances.

And they finally learned the meaning of his words:

"As I have loved you,
so must you love one another."   Jn 13:34

It's obvious that the years
with him
had made a great difference
in the lives of the Twelve.

They "went back to Jerusalem
filled with great joy
and spent all their time in the Temple
giving thanks to God."   Lk 24:52-53

"And they gathered frequently
to pray as a group
together with the women,
and with Mary the mother of Jesus,
and his brothers."   Ac 1:14

They also chose Matthias to replace Judas.   Ac 1:26

For nine day days they prepared themselves
for the Teacher's Successor,
the Holy Spirit,
who would teach them everything
and make them remember
all that he had taught them.   Jn 14:26

121

And NOW
as we assess our teaching . . .

✧ The true test of learning
    certainly can't be determined
      by a five-point quiz
        at the end of a forty-minute lesson,
          or a four-page test
            after a few weeks' study of a topic.

   Learning
     that makes a difference in lives
       must penetrate much deeper
         than the surface information
         skimmed from books,
             which coats the outer layers of the mind.

✧ What's the use of drilling verb tenses,
    sentence sense, and punctuation marks,
      if we haven't taught our students
        how to communicate
          in honesty,
            in truth,
              and in love?

✧ What's the purpose of having them
    speeding through country-capital associations,
      if we haven't taught them
        to love,
          appreciate,
            and accept
              other cultures and peoples?

✧ Why spend time checking memorized prayers,
    if we haven't taught them
        how to pray—
          to speak to God from their heart
          and to listen to him?

✧ What's the use of teaching them
to name every human bone and muscle,
if we haven't taught them to respect life
in its every stage and form?

✧ Why teach them
every type of investment and means of profit,
if they don't know
the relative value of all things material,
if they aren't generous
with what they have?

✧ What's the value of being able to recognize
every major work of every notable artist
and composer,
if they can't appreciate all forms of beauty
and all effort exerted to produce it?

✧ What's the point of developing intellectual geniuses,
if we haven't taught them
to be grateful for their own gifts
and to be kind,
respectful
and helpful
to those with lesser talents?

* * *　　　* * *　　　* * *

The real test of learning
comes after the teacher and students
are separated
by the space of years
and then by the gulf between time and eternity.

What will our students
be doing
with their lives
to improve their world?

Storytelling Techniques

Jesus was a born storyteller.
He seemed to tell stories most often
 when he was with small groups;
  sometimes among friends
  but occasionally with his enemies.

He wove attention holding plots
 around some fascinating characters
  in recognizable settings
   for his audience.

And he was a master
 at drawing the theme from his students.

The Good Samaritan	Lk 10:25-37
The Two Sons	Mt 21:28-32

The evangelists recorded many instances
 where he simply told the story,
  concluded with the moral,
   and left the application
    in the hands of the listeners.

The Pharisee and the Tax Collector	Lk 18:9-14
The Workers in the Vineyard	Mt 20:1-16
The Lost Sheep	Lk 15:4-7
Parable of the Rich Fool	Lk 12:16-21

Occasionally
 he even left the interpretation of the moral
  to his audience:

The Lost Son	Lk 15:11-32
The Rich Man and Lazarus	Lk 16:19-31
Parable of the Gold Coin	Lk 19:12-27

But he made certain
    that Simon the Pharisee
        didn't miss the implication
            about the moneylender and his two debtors.
                                        Lk 7:36-50

* * *   * * *   * * *

And it's a good thing
    the disciples weren't very sharp
        at grasping some of his stories.
Thanks to their openness
    in asking for further explanations,
        he gave detailed interpretations
        of some thought provoking parables:

The Sower and the Seed	Lk 8:11-15
The Widow and the Judge	Lk 18:1-8
The Shrewd Manager	Lk 16:1-13
The Wheat and the Weeds	Mt 13:24-30, 36-43

*Effective use of both inductive and deductive teaching
with stories!*

And NOW
as we assess our storytelling . . .

✧ A story related to a lesson can come from your personal
experience, the Bible, folklore, the news, or a book.

✧ Storytelling can address classroom issues and promote
discussion without embarrassing any student.

✧ Reading a story aloud can introduce a topic, relax
students after an intense study, and motivate them to
develop a habit of daily reading.

Students In Trouble

He'd created a bit of havoc
    in the life of the man born blind
      by curing him.

The man had to begin his sight-life
    by facing people
      who doubted his identity,
      and requested a continuous
      and tiring retelling
      of how it had all happened
         — neighbors, strangers, Pharisees.

Even his parents were put on the spot:

"How is it that he can see?"

"He is old enough; ask him."

The fellow must have thought the episode
    a closed issue
    after his firm support
      for the man who "came from God,"
and his own subsequent expulsion
      from the synagogue.

But it was then
    that the Teacher came back.

The action of the healing Teacher
    had started all the man's problems,
so the concerned Teacher
    returned to calm the scene
      and reward him
        as only he could do.   Jn 9:1-41

         * * *   * * *   * * *

Jesus never hesitated to defend his Twelve
when they were criticized unjustly.

— On a Sabbath day
the hungry disciples munched on wheat heads
that they picked
as they walked through the field.

When the indignant Pharisees
were scandalized at such Sabbath-abuse,
Jesus defended the Twelve
with a reference to the great King David,
and set the accusers straight
about the Sabbath.   Mt 12:1-8

— When eyebrows were raised
about his disciples' eating and drinking
while disciples of others fasted,
Jesus explained their actions
with his bridegroom parable.   Lk 5:33-35

— The Pharisees also questioned
the disciples' eating
without properly washing their hands.
And Jesus counter-questioned them,

"And why do you disobey God's command
and follow your own teaching?"   Mt 15:1-3

— Once his followers were even accused
of being too noisy
as they rejoiced at his approach to Jerusalem.
(And what K–12 teacher hasn't heard the same!)
His response?

"If they keep quiet, I tell you,
the stones themselves will start shouting." Lk 19 37-40

— He even worked a miracle
　　　to protect Peter
　　　　　from facing the consequence
　　　　　of an impulsive swing of the sword.
　　(Great motive, wrong action!)　　Jn 18:10-11; Lk 22:49-51

Twice, he defended Mary,
　　　　　the sister of Martha and Lazarus.
　　　　　— once when she preferred
　　　　　　　listening at his feet
　　　　　　　to housekeeping tasks for his visit. Lk 10:38-41
　　　　　— and once when she was extravagant
　　　　　　　with a pint of perfume
　　　　　　　which she poured over his feet.　　Jn 12:1-7
Both times he came to her rescue.
Her attention to him was rewarded.

And NOW
when our students are in trouble . . .

✧ Students need to know their teacher will come
　　　　　to their defense if they are unjustly accused.

　　　　　And if they are guilty,
　　　　　they need to know even more that
　　　　　　　their teacher will be just as present
　　　　　　　with support and advice.

✧ We must be present to our students
　　　　　according to their needs.

　　　　— He told his Twelve:
　　　　　"I do not call you servants.
　　　　　. . . Instead I call you friends."　　Jn 15:15

128

PART EIGHT

A LOOK AT HIS TEACHERS: MARY AND JOSEPH OF NAZARETH

Mary

A LOOK AT HIS TEACHERS:
MARY AND JOSEPH OF NAZARETH

It's been said
    that teachers tend to teach
    the way they were taught
        when they were children,
        rather than how
        they were taught to teach.

If that's true,
    then it should be enlightening
        to look at the two persons
        who shaped the Teacher's habits,
            ideals, and values during his early life.

Of all the humans he could have chosen
    to compose his human family,
        he selected plain, simple folk who lived by faith:
        Mary and Joseph of Nazareth.

When the Nazarenes
    were trying to determine
        the source of his wisdom,
    they asked:
        "Isn't he the carpenter's son?
        Isn't Mary his mother?
        . . . Where did he get all this?"   Mk 6:2-5

And they rejected him.

Evidently,
    the carpenter and his wife hadn't been outstanding,
    and there was nothing noteworthy
        about their education.
                so, whence his?

Mary of Nazareth

The evangelists give us some clues
    about what he must have learned from her.

— She must have shared with her all-knowing Son
    the story of her wholehearted willingness
    to be the Lord's servant.   Lk 1:35-38

— He surely knew about his mother's
    three-month visit
    to assist her elderly cousin
        before his own birth.   Lk 1:39-56

— He'd been aware of her respect for
    and compliance with the Law each year
    as the family made the annual
    Passover feast journey to Jerusalem.   Lk 2:41

— He easily would recall
    his mother's straightforward reaction
    to his prolonged Temple visit
    when he was twelve:

        "Son, why have you done this to us?
        Your father and I
            have been terribly worried
            trying to find you."   Lk 2:42-52

      * * *   * * *   * * *

During his first thirty years
    she'd grown to know him well enough
    to be certain
        that if she made him aware of a problem,
        he'd try do something about it.

So,
   at Cana's wedding of the season,
      she found it necessary
      to speak only ten words,
         — five to him:
           "They are out of wine."

         — five to the servants:
           "Do whatever he tells you."

She knew that he would take some action

   Wanting to do what she could to help,
      she did some front-running for him.

And nothing more
   is mentioned about her
   on this occasion,
      except that after the reception
   she accompanied her son,
      his disciples, and some relatives
         for a few days' stay in Capernaum.   Jn 2:1-12

         * * *   * * *   * * *

She visited him
   at least once while he was teaching,
   but no details are given
      about their meeting.

When her presence was announced,
   Jesus claimed that his mother and brothers
      were those who do what the Father wants.

This might sound
like a putdown of his biological mother,
      until we realize
      who better than Mary
carried out the Father's will?   Mt 12:46-48

Courageously she stood close to Jesus' cross
— when the sight of her
  would afford him some support.   Jn 19:25

And in his dying moments
 he took care of his mother,
   his friend,
    his teacher
 by entrusting her
  to the beloved disciple.
And from that hour, the disciple
took her into his own home.   Jn 19:26-27

    * * *   * * *   * * *

Luke mentions her by name
 one final time in his Acts of the Apostles
  recording how she
   was among the little band
  of his followers
  who went to pray as a group.   Ac 1:14

And on Pentecost she, the Spouse of the Holy Spirit,
 was filled with her son's Spirit
 to mother his church.   Ac 2:1-4

    * * *   * * *   * * *

From all that's recorded of her,
 his teacher seemed to have been
   . . . simple and unassuming
   . . . devoutly religious
   . . . very economical with words
   . . . able to instill confidence
   . . . a loving woman,
     concerned about others' needs
   . . . accepting of his friends and his mission
   . . . interested in his mission
     without being interfering.

Joseph of Nazareth

And what do we know about this man
    whom the neighbors assumed
        was the father of Jesus?

Joseph of Nazareth was
    — a man of deep faith
        who recognized divine inspiration
        and direction
            even in his sleep!   Mt 1:18-23; 2:13; 19-22

    — a man of action
        who lost no time in responding
        to that inspiration.   Mt 1:24-25; 2:14; 21-23

    — a sensitive man
        who, when he did not know Who lived
            within his fiancée,
        planned to break their engagement
            secretly.   Mt 1:19

    — the host of one-of-a-kind receptions,
        who was just as comfortable
            with important wise men from the East
            as he was with the poor from the fields.
                Lk 2:1-20; Mt 2:1-12

    — a man knowledgeable of geography
        who carefully planned journeys for his family
        — the round trip from Nazareth to Bethlehem
        and back to Nazareth,
        with a shrewd layover in Egypt.   Mt 2:13-14

    — the capable guide and instructor
        of the young carpenter
        who under his guidance
            developed skill with the tools of his trade,
                and habits of honesty and industriousness,
                    as he grew in wisdom, age and grace
                        before God and men.

135

* * *   * * *   * * *

The influence of Mary and Joseph was obvious.
Throughout his life, the Master Teacher
was noted for all the characteristics
he had absorbed from the two most important humans
in his young life.

**And NOW
as we teach his children
and young people . . .**

✧ Be aware that our students are not only observing
who we are
and what we do
and what we stand for.

They tend to reflect our characteristics,
our attitudes and values.

✧ An occasional personal evaluation
might keep us mindful
of the significance of our role.

PART NINE

QUALITIES OF THE MASTER TEACHER

The Paralytic

QUALITIES OF THE MASTER TEACHER

Although the only personal qualities
   the Teacher specifically told the disciples
   they should learn from him
      were gentleness and humility,   Mt 11:29
      he gave ample evidence
      of possessing many more traits
         that are worthy of imitation
         by any teacher.

* * *   * * *   * * *

> **He was gentle, respectful, and forgiving**
   with those who had surrendered to a misguided heart:
    . . . the woman caught in adultery,
    . . . the one who had five husbands,
    . . . Mary, the prostitute.
   forgiving the action, but not condoning it.
   "Go but do not sin again."   Jn 8:11

> **He was concerned about his students' families**
   — even mothers–in–law!   Lk 4:38-39

> **He made his students feel important.**
   — He called them salt and light.   Mt 5:13-16
   — He accepted an invitation
      to dinner with outcasts
         to honor a new student.   Mt 9:9-13

> **He was protective of his students' reputations**
   — even in his contacts with Judas.   Jn 13:27-30
   — His Good Shepherd parable was told
      to reassure the tax collectors
         and outcasts who listened to him.   Lk 15:1-7

> **He was prayerful.**
>> — He began his teaching mission
>>> with a forty-day retreat.   Lk 4:1-13
>> — He spent many nights in prayer
>>> in lonely places.

> **He was an inspiration to his students.**
>> —"Lord teach us to pray."   Lk 11:1

> **He was tender and loving**
>> with the apostles
>> and Mary Magdalene
>>> immediately after his resurrection,
>>> as he led them from the shock of grief
>>>> to accepting the astounding miracle
>>>> of his rising . . . and
>>>> to the realization that he was leaving them
>>>>> with a God-sized mission to accomplish.

> **He knew men's hearts.**
>> — "There was no need
>>> for anyone to tell him about men,
>>> because he knew
>>>> what was in their hearts."   Jn 2:25

> **He was cautious not to teach too much,
> too soon.**
>> — "I have much more to tell you,
>>> *but now* it would be too much
>>> for you to bear."   Jn 16:12

> **He was perceptive.**
>> — He was aware of his student's needs
>>> before the student expressed them.   Lk 10:10-13
>> — He answered questions that his students
>>> were too embarrassed to ask.   Jn 16:17-19
>> — He didn't force an answer
>>> when he knew they were ashamed
>>> to tell the truth.   Mk 9: 32-33

> **He was patient**
with slower students
and their naive questions.
During his last supper with them,
as he referred to his "going,"
they asked "Where?"   Jn 13:36;14:5
But sometimes his frustration showed,
as when the disciples were worried
about having bread.
He scolded them
by seven rapid-fire questions   Mt 16:8-11

> **He started his teaching
at his students' readiness point.**
no matter how elementary:
— "What are you looking for?"
— "Where do you live, teacher?"
— "Come, and see."
. . . and he moved them forward.   Jn 1:35-39

> **He explained clearly with simple examples.**
— "A man is born physically of human parents,
but he is born spiritually of the Spirit."

— The wind...it is like that with everyone
who is born of the Spirit."

— "The light has come into the world,
but people love the darkness."   Jn 3:1-21

> **He prepared them adequately for the final exam.**
— telling them precisely
what questions to expect
and how to answer them!   Mt 25:31-46

> **He was thorough.**
— When the almost–cured blind man described people
as "trees walking around",
Jesus finished the job and
— "he saw all things clearly."   Mk 8:22-26

> **He searched for the best way to explain.**
— "What shall we say the Kingdom of God is like"?
— "What parable shall we use to explain it?"   Mk 4:30

> **He was practical.**
He noticed details overlooked by others.
— When the stunned crowd stood gaping
at Lazarus,
still bound up in his burial sheets
at the entrance of his tomb,
Jesus told them,
"Untie him and let him go."   Jn 11:44
— When Jairus' young daughter
was called back from the dead
he "ordered them
to give her something to eat."   Lk 8:55

> **He was knowledgeable about his subject matter.**
— "When the crowds heard this
they were amazed at his teaching."   Mt 22:33

— "He taught with authority."   Mt 7:29

— "All the people kept listening to him,
not wanting to miss a single word."   Lk 19:48

> **He was available**
— to the crowds   Mk 4:33
— to those who needed his healing power   Mk 1:32-34
— when he prayed all night
and in the early morning hours
to leave the day free for his ministry.

He seemed to have no office-hour limitations!

> **He was prudently cautious.**
— disappearing in the midst of the crowd
who wanted to throw him over the cliff,   Lk 4:28-30
— choosing not to "go openly" when he knew
the timing wasn't right

142

* * *　　　* * *　　　* * *

An outstanding quality
　　of the Master Teacher
　　　　was his adamant stand
　　　　　　on specific issues of morality.

He expected his students
　　to live
　　according to a clear-cut code of action,
　　based on strong beliefs.
So he explained those principles
　　in definite, precise language;
　　　　he answered questions about them
　　　　to clarify misunderstandings;
　　　　　　and he applied them to daily life.

Most importantly,
　　It was evident that he lived what he taught
　　　　— about anger　　　　　　　　　　　Mt 5:21-26
　　　　— about judging others　　　　　　　　Mt 7:1-5
　　　　— about love of enemies　　　　　　　Mt 5:43-48
　　　　— about performing religious acts in public　Mt 6:1-4
　　　　— about prayer　　　　Mt 6:5-15; 7:7-12; Lk 11:5-13
　　　　— about revenge　　　　　　　　　　Mt 5:38-42

　　His position was just as unyielding
　　　　on the current issues of his time:
　　　　— on the Law　　　　　　　　　　　Mt 5:17-20
　　　　— on adultery　　　　　　　　　　　Mt 5:27-28
　　　　— on divorce　　　　Mt 5:31-32; 19:1-10; Mk 10:2-12
　　　　— on fasting　　　　　　　　　　　Mt 6:16-18
　　　　— on material wealth　　　　Mt 6:19-21; Lk 12:22-34

143

* * *   * * *   * * *

The Teacher
    was revolutionary in his teachings.

He demanded
    far more that than the minimum requirements
       of the Law.

And he made no apologies for it.

       You have heard that it was said . . .
         but now I tell you . . .

And NOW
when we examine our own qualities . . .

✧ Our students deserve to see
    what is in store for them
       if they follow our teaching.

    We are that best example.

✧ The principles we give our students
       must flow from solid beliefs.

    Consequently, those principles
      must be broad enough
         to become the foundation
           for the structure of daily living,
    and clear enough
         to give a dependable sense of direction
           in matters that fluctuate and develop
           in our changing society.

✧ We need to teach them

... how to think
... how to raise questions
... how to offer opinions
... how to read and listen
... how to speak and write
... how to evaluate
... how to come to valid conclusions
... how and when to lead
... how and when to follow

And we need to provide
many opportunities to practice
all these lessons on all levels
preschool through university.

— The facts the students practice
may appear to be simple or unimportant.
they may even become obsolete!

But the HOW-TO skills they develop
will grow stronger
... ready to serve them
in the future.

PART TEN

TEACHER

TEACHER

He could have chosen any planet
    in any of the countless solar systems
      he had designed

       . . . but he chose ours,
        and he spent thirty-three years with us.

He could have chosen any period
    in our earth-history
      as the most effective one
       for spreading his Good News.

       . . . But he chose a time
        before so many innovative inventions
         were even imagined
           — before satellite communication
           — before television
           — before computers
           — before electricity
           — even before printing!

       . . . But he chose a time
        when his original team of messengers
        could travel only on foot
        or by ox-cart,
         or by sea-vessels powered
          by men's muscles.

He could have chosen any place
    as his headquarters:
    Rome, Corinth, Antioch, Alexandria
      — all progressive ancient cities,
        when he came,
or a continent not yet discovered
in the years B.C.

    . . . But he chose to spend thirty years
      of preparation in a no-place: Nazareth
      and "Can anything good come from Nazareth?"

He could have spent his final years
    as a statesman
        influencing governments and world powers
    as a physician,
       curing all the diseases of his time
    as a renowned social reformer,
       founding a whole new social system.

    . . . But he chose to be a Teacher
      — to mold characters
      — to shape human destinies
      — to influence families
      — to affect future generations
      — to influence neighborhoods,
          cities,
            nations,
              the world
      — to spread the Kingdom of his Father.

He closed his time on earth
    by directing his followers:

    "Go to the whole world
    and preach the Gospel to all mankind."   Mk 16:15

And they did.

His disciples' disciples multiplied
again and again and again,
and are still motivated by his promise:

"I will be with you always
to the end of the age." Mt 28:20

And they spend their days teaching,
inspired by the life,
the message,
and
the methods
of Jesus,
the Master Teacher.

About the Author

Sister Regina Alfonso, originally from Memphis, Tennessee, moved to Ohio in order to join the Sisters of Notre Dame. She began her teaching ministry in elementary schools in Ohio, Virginia, and Washington, D.C. That experience was a valuable preparation for her next ministry in teacher education at Notre Dame College of Ohio. A veteran educator, she frequently gave workshops and presentations on teaching, even traveling to Uganda, Africa, to teach new methods to teachers. She also worked on a religion textbook series.

In 1973, Sister Regina began designing learning games intended to reinforce math and reading skills. By 1990, she was conducting make-and-take sessions to share her ideas with her teacher education students and local faculties. She now has more than sixty games for children in grades K to 5.

While teaching at Notre Dame College, Sister Regina undertook the project of updating the libraries of urban Catholic schools, an activity she continued after she retired—until twenty schools benefited from her volunteer work. After retiring, Sister engaged in tutoring and preparing adults for GED testing. Most recently, besides working on this book, she is tutoring children from grades K to 2.

Sister is seldom seen without a crochet hook in her hand. For the Notre Dame Sisters' annual boutiques, she produces unique creations—such as animals, dolls, and nursery rhyme characters. She also crochets booties, caps, and blankets for the babies in Le Bonheur's Children's Hospital in Memphis.

Sister Regina currently resides at the Notre Dame Provincial Center in Chardon, Ohio.

Dear Joyce,

I went to dinner
at a restaurant at Notre
Dame + we had
dinner. She later
went + we hung in
then. She pretended
this work + we were
the first to purchase
one. I love the picture
of it. I hope her
before the weather

Please me come
take her to lunch!
I hope all is well
with you. We need
to catch up!

Love
Renne

Made in the USA
Middletown, DE
18 February 2017